Go, Johnny, Go!

Go, Johnny Go!

Paul O'Flynn

Gill Books

e

/2

gillbooks.ie

Books is an imprint of M.H. Gill and Co.

ext © Paul O'Flynn 2020

978 07171 8976 2

Designed by Westchester Publishing Services
Print origination by O'K Graphic Design, Dublin
Proofread by Jane Rogers
Printed by Replika Press Pvt. Ltd., India

This book is typeset in 12/18 pt Tahoma.

The paper used in this book comes from the wood pulp of managed forests. For every tree felled, at least one tree is planted, thereby renewing natural resources.

All rights reserved.

No part of this publication may be copied, reproduced or transmitted in any form or by any means, without written permission of the publishers.

A CIP catalogue record for this book is available from the British Library.

5 4 3

Author's Note

This book is based on Johnny Sexton's life and career. It would be impossible for me to go back in time and listen in to all of the conversations with Johnny that have taken place over the years, so I have had to imagine them. I also haven't actually been in the dressing rooms or Johnny's home or inside his head, because that would just be weird. However, all of the scores and matches are real and all of Johnny's achievements mentioned in the book are factual. He really is that amazing.

About the author

Paul O'Flynn is an RTÉ News and Sport presenter and journalist. A graduate of DCU, with a BA in Journalism and an MA in International Relations, he is also an associate lecturer at his alma mater. He is a keen sportsperson and amateur swimmer, and in 2018 he was the winner of the Liffey Swim.

Chapter 1

Drop goal

They could hear the brass band playing from deep inside the stadium. Drums drumming, trumpets trumpeting and French fans singing along. The excitement was building in the Stade de France in Paris. It was a dark, wet winter's day, just a few minutes to kick-off. The start of the 2018 Six Nations: France v Ireland.

Johnny looked around the dressing room. He knew this place well but he never liked it. Ireland never liked it. They had won games here just twice in almost 40 years. Paris was a graveyard for Irish rugby dreams. But this year was different. Johnny could feel it.

Go, Johnny, Go!

Ireland were one of the best teams in the world by now and they feared nobody. They had their sights set on winning the Grand Slam, the almost impossible task of beating England, Wales, Scotland and France in just one season. They had only managed to do this twice in over 100 years.

Johnny fiddled with his socks a little, looked up and scanned the room. His eyes settled on Rory Best, Ireland's inspiring captain and leader on the pitch, lacing up his boots. He looked across to Rob Kearney, one of the best full backs to ever play for Ireland. The Munster magician Keith Earls was jumping on his toes. There was a new crop of young stars, too, like James Ryan, Jacob Stockdale and Dan Leavy. They were nervous but excited about what lay ahead. Coach Joe Schmidt quietly dished out some last-minute instructions. He was the tough teacher from New Zealand who had transformed Irish rugby.

Then came the referee's knock on the door. It was time. They all stopped and turned

Drop goal

towards Johnny, their star out-half. The team's driving force and playmaker. The best number 10 in the world, with all the skills and a will to win to match.

'Let's go, boys!' he roared.

Fireworks crackled as they walked up the tunnel and out onto the pitch. The small pockets of Irish fans who had travelled to Paris tried to make themselves heard, but they were mostly drowned out by the French. Almost 75,000 fans packed in to the stadium for what was sure to be a classic. Little did they know that they were about to see one of the greatest moments in the history of the game.

Johnny stood still for the anthems. This was always a special moment, no matter how many times he played for Ireland. He stared out with steely black eyes, taking it all in, pride rising inside him as he thought to himself, 'We're not losing today.'

The referee blew his whistle and game was on. The roar of the crowd sent a shiver down Johnny's back. He was up and running and

Go, Johnny, Go!

already barking out orders to his teammates. He got his hands on the ball early with a lovely pass to set Stockdale free. It didn't take long before Ireland had a penalty. His first shot on goal in the Six Nations.

Johnny's heart had been racing, his blood pumping and sweat pouring. Now it was time to slow down and keep calm. He had a routine he practised since he was a little boy. Place the ball on the tee. Line up the kick. Look at the posts and then back down to the ball. Think about the distance, the wind, the rain. Pick the spot where you want it to go. Put your foot under the ball, then take a few steps back. Breathe. Picture it going over the bar. A few steps on his tippy-toes. Start the run-up and swing your boot right through the ball. It was perfect. Straight between the posts.

A superb kick from Sexton. Ireland are in front!

Scrum-half Conor Murray gave him a nod. 'Nice one, Sexto. Keep them coming!'

It was a bruising battle in the heavy rain. Ireland's forwards were working hard and

Drop goal

getting the better of France. Johnny took full advantage and added kick after kick. By half-time, the men in green were 9-3 ahead.

They stretched their lead in the second half, to 12-3. Ireland looked on course for victory. But France were always dangerous. Johnny knew that more than most.

'Keep working, boys. Don't give them an inch,' he shouted from behind the scrum, clapping his hands to encourage them. He was always instructing his teammates and calling the play. But the next kick went to the French and the gap was closing. The home fans roared with delight. The noise was deafening as the stars sparkled in the Paris night sky.

Then things got even worse.

From nowhere France came up with a bit of magic. Flying winger Teddy Thomas threw the ball to Belleau, who fired it straight back to Thomas. It was quick thinking. Ireland were in trouble. Murray tried to tackle but Thomas flew past him before twisting inside Stockdale.

Go, Johnny, Go!

'No, no, no,' thought Johnny. He ran like his life depended on it to stop them. But it was too late. Thomas slid over the line and France were in front. The fans went wild singing 'Allez les Bleus'! 'Come on the Blues!'

With just minutes to go, Ireland's Grand Slam dreams looked over before they had even started. The Irish players were starting to drop their heads. They looked beaten. All except Johnny. He refused to give up, grabbing the ball and running back to the halfway line to restart. What he did next would be remembered forever.

Johnny pinged a perfect ball right into the hands of Iain Henderson. It started a remarkable play that would go on for more than 5 minutes. Ireland used up every ounce of their energy, trying to squeeze out inch after inch. Player after player took on the ball and tried to drive through the French wall. C. J. Stander, Bundee Aki, Peter O'Mahony. Johnny was roaring them on all the time. But the French defence stood firm.

Drop goal

Johnny could see that Ireland were getting nowhere. He thought about a cross-field kick. Was it too risky? 'Those who dare, win,' he thought. He spotted Keith Earls in some space out wide and launched a perfect kick right into his arms. It could have been all over but Earls gathered it and Ireland were off again. Pick and go. Pick and go. Surely France would eventually run out of steam.

But it was Ireland who were running out of time. The clock was in the red. Already 80 minutes had passed and their chance was slipping away. Johnny's leg was cramping. He was running on empty, so he stepped back and stopped to stretch it. The French thought he was trying to fool them, but Johnny had nothing left in the tank. He knew there was only one chance left. He would have to go for a drop goal. But they were miles out.

His partnership with scrum-half Murray was so tight that they didn't even need to speak. Murray knew from Johnny's body language. He knew they needed to get just a little closer.

Go, Johnny, Go!

Ireland hit a thumping ruck and suddenly had some space. They were now 3 minutes, 42 seconds into overtime, but Johnny looked up and gave Murray a flick of the eyebrows. That was all he needed. Murray scooped up the ball and fired a fizzing pass right into Johnny's hands. Then time seemed to slow down.

Everybody could see what Johnny was going to do. The French players charged forward with their hands in the air to block the kick. The fans in the stadium couldn't believe their eyes. He's too far out, surely? He was 42 metres out, to be precise. One of the longest drop goals anyone had ever attempted. Everybody back home in Ireland, watching on TV, held their breath. Hearts stopped. It all happened in slow motion. Johnny had only half a second, even less. He released the ball and swung his boot with all the force he had.

Sexton shows his guts and goes for glory!

He gave the ball an almighty thump. The players froze. All they could do was watch.

Drop goal

The egg-shaped ball flew high into the sky and started to spin. Once, twice, three times. It was on target, alright. Johnny knew that straight away. But did it have the distance? It was dropping, dropping, dropping. Johnny's eyes bulged in disbelief.

It's going towards the posts. It's over! Ireland with the drop goal. *Le drop*! **France have been destroyed with the final kick of the game. Ireland have snatched it!**

Johnny stretched out his arms wide and pumped his fists in the air. He couldn't believe it. He'd done it. One of the greatest kicks of all time. His teammates ran towards him and bundled him to the ground. Murray, Kearney and Robbie Henshaw were the first to pile on. Johnny was smothered at the bottom. He could hardly breathe but he didn't care. It was his greatest moment on the rugby field. The French players were shell-shocked, lying bloodied and exhausted, with their heads in their hands.

Go, Johnny, Go!

When Johnny finally surfaced, Bundee jumped straight into his arms. 'Yes, Sexto! How do you do it, bro?'

'What a cracker!' Joe Schmidt laughed. 'We knew you had that in your locker.'

Johnny was on top of the world. It got even better over the next few weeks. Ireland beat Italy, Wales, Scotland and then England on St Patrick's Day, winning the Grand Slam. History had been made.

Ireland's Grand Slam story started with 'le drop goal' on that famous night in Paris. But the story of their hero Johnny Sexton started a long time before that. Johnny's story started back in 1985, in a place called Rathgar on the southside of Dublin.

Chapter 2

Rathgar

Thursday, 11 July 1985, was a famous day for Irish rugby. Jonathan Jeremiah Sexton was born. He was the first baby for his parents, Jerry and Clare. They were so in love with their beautiful son. He already had a head of jet-black hair. His brown eyes were so dark they were like little lumps of coal.

'I can't stop looking at him!' Jerry said, with a big smile on his face.

'I know,' said his mam, as she kissed him on top of his head. 'He's beautiful. My little baby boy.'

'What should we call him?' asked his dad.

Go, Johnny, Go!

'How about Jonathan?' asked his mam. 'He looks like a Jonathan.'

The little baby opened his eyes, smiled and wriggled his legs.

'That's it settled, then, I suppose,' laughed his mam.

'Look! He's already kicking his little legs,' said his dad, with excitement in his voice. He leaned over and whispered into baby Johnny's ear. 'Maybe you'll grow up to play for Ireland one day.'

Johnny's family were already big rugby fans and players. His dad had grown up in Listowel, County Kerry, and later moved to Dublin, where he studied in UCD. He worked as an accountant when he finished college, but that was just his day job. Rugby was his true passion. He was always a proud Munster man. He was even an amateur international scrum-half, who played for Bective, near their home in Dublin. His brother Willie, Johnny's uncle, was a strong forward who played for Garryowen, Munster and even three times for Ireland.

Rathgar

Johnny's mam was a Dub and her four brothers all played rugby, too. She was a very good golfer herself. It's no wonder Johnny was born with sporting talent.

Rugby fever had gripped the country around the time Johnny was born. Just months before, Ireland had won the Triple Crown. They had done it in style, too. It started with a brilliant second-half performance to come from behind and beat Scotland. Next came Ireland's first win against Wales in almost 20 years. It had all come down to a decider against England in Dublin. Johnny's mam was pacing around the house, five months pregnant. She was trying not to get too tense as the excitement built.

Brendan Mullin has charged it down. The ball's over the line. If he can fall on it …

It's a try! A try for Ireland!

But England had fought back. The game was right in the balance as the clock ticked down. Johnny's mam, like everybody else in Ireland, could hardly handle the nerves.

Go, Johnny, Go!

Ireland now with the last-ditch attack. The last minute of play. Back comes Bradley. Bradley to Kiernan. Drop goal on. Drop goal tried. Drop goal good! Three points! Ireland have won the Triple Crown!

The crowd at Lansdowne Road erupted. People celebrated all over the country. It was one of the greatest moments in Irish rugby. In their home in Rathgar, Dublin, the excitement seeped into Johnny's mam and her baby boy not yet born. Little did anyone know that when he grew up, 33 years later, he would kick an even more famous drop goal wearing the green shirt of Ireland.

Chapter 3

Munster blood

Johnny was spoiled rotten when he was small. He got all the attention. But he wasn't on his own for long. Soon his sister Gillian was born. Then came two brothers, Mark and Jerry Junior. They were all sports mad and competitive with each other. Johnny was a shy child, but that all changed when it came to sport. From the minute he was born, he hated losing. He had a temper, too, which he blamed on his Munster blood.

By the age of four, Johnny was already a firm fixture at Bective Rugby Club. His dad played a game every Sunday. Johnny loved to tag along and watch his dad play. His dad

Go, Johnny, Go!

was a big, powerful scrum-half. He liked a bit of rough and tumble with the opposition. One time, Johnny's dad broke his nose while playing. There was blood everywhere, but his dad wasn't afraid. This is something Johnny would share as he got older. He would cheer on his dad and his Bective teammates from the sidelines. As soon as the game was finished, Johnny would shoot off to practise what he had just seen.

In Johnny's mind, he was the star out-half playing alongside his dad. He would throw the ball into the air, catch it, run across the pitch and jump over an imaginary try line.

Johnny Sexton has done it again! He's won the match for Bective!

He would play the commentary in his head.

When he got a little older, the whole family would come along. His sister Gillian wasn't much into rugby, but all the boys were. They would have epic matches on the green in front of the Bective clubhouse. They would knock lumps out of each other, pretending to play

Munster blood

against one of Bective's big rivals. Old Wesley, Wanderers, Belvedere or Lansdowne.

The Sexton brothers could almost make up the spine of a team by themselves. Johnny was the playmaker. He had silky skills, great kicking, passing and vision. Mark was a strong centre. He was as fast as lightning. If he whizzed past you'd never catch him. Then there was Jerry Junior. Even though he was the youngest, he was always going to grow up to be the biggest. He was a powerful forward, like their uncle Willie. If he hit you with a tackle you'd know all about it. They had so much fun together.

Sometimes their games went on long past dark. The brothers would play in the faint flicker of the floodlights, or the glow from the windows of the clubhouse. They almost always ignored calls from their parents to come in for a bite to eat or to go home. On days when it rained, they would slip inside the clubhouse to the ballroom, even though it was against the rules. Someone would keep lookout so they wouldn't be caught. It was a great place for a kick-about.

Go, Johnny, Go!

One day they were right in the heart of battle. Johnny and his brothers were playing against some other boys and girls from the club. It was an epic contest and the result was right in the balance. Jerry made a big tackle and turned over the ball. He quickly got his hands on it and popped it up to Mark. He ran like the wind through the gap before fizzing a pass to Johnny.

'Go on, Johnny!' shouted Mark. 'Finish it!'

But one of the bigger boys charged towards him.

'Uh oh,' thought Johnny. 'I'm about to get hit!'

With some clever, quick thinking, Johnny decided to put boot to ball. He connected much harder than he meant. He gave it a right wallop. Suddenly the ball was flying high into the air, right towards the ceiling. All the boys and girls stopped and stared.

Smash!

The ball crashed straight into the lights. Glass shattered everywhere.

Munster blood

'What's going on in here?' roared one of the grown-ups, running in to see what had happened.

Johnny had some explaining to do. 'It was an accident,' he muttered.

Johnny looked up in disbelief. He was in big trouble. They all were. He thought he was going to be punished. Maybe he wouldn't be allowed play rugby for a week.

Thankfully for Johnny and his brothers, their dad saw the funny side. Rather than get angry, he was secretly happy his little boys shared his love of rugby.

Before long, Johnny was playing his first proper match in an organised sevens game. He was wearing a jersey that was way too big for him. Bective's famous red, green and white hoops, hanging down past his knees. It didn't bother Johnny at all. In fact, he won a medal that he still cherishes to this day. It was already clear that he had lots of talent and could be a future star.

Go, Johnny, Go!

Even though Johnny was born in the heart of rugby country, on the south side of Dublin, he had Munster blood in him. He loved going to Kerry to meet his relations, especially his Nana Brenda. She lived in a house on the main street in the town of Listowel. Her front room was a shop, where she sold children's clothes. Johnny loved sitting in the back room by the fire. Sometimes his nana would bring in customers to see him. She spoiled him and he loved it. It was always his favourite place to go and get away from everything. Especially when he grew up and needed a break from rugby.

His godfather Billy also lived in the heart of the town. He was a son of the famous writer John B. Keane, who also ran a well-known bar on the main street. Johnny spent many days there, hanging around the back, kicking a ball against the wall. John B. would be giving out inside.

'When is that young fella going back to Dublin?' he'd ask. 'We might be able to get some peace!'

Munster blood

Even though he was only starting out in rugby, Johnny was already dreaming of playing for Ireland someday. He let godfather Billy know all about it.

'Billy, when I grow up and play for Ireland, can I hang my jersey on the wall in the bar? I'll sign it for you!'

Everyone laughed except Johnny. He was serious.

Those early days in Kerry stayed with Johnny forever. No matter how much he loved sport, his family always came first. He may have been a true-blue Leinster man on the outside, but inside, the red blood of Munster flowed deep in his veins.

Chapter 4
Will to win

Johnny always wanted everything he did to be perfect. Whether it was in school, on the golf course, playing soccer or rugby, he made sure to get everything right. Practising hard was the only way. His mam and dad always encouraged him to do his best at whatever he did. But Johnny didn't need much of a push. He was so competitive. He didn't like to lose.

One day Johnny was out in the garden playing keepie-uppies with a football. His dad watched him from the window, smiling as Johnny kept going until he had mastered the skill.

Will to win

'Hey, Johnny!' his dad shouted. 'Bet you can't do 300 in a row!'

'No way!' said Johnny. 'I'm not Roy Keane!'

Johnny was a huge Manchester United fan by now. He'd been hooked ever since Ireland had got to the quarter-finals of the World Cup in 1990. Keano was his favourite player. Johnny admired not just his football skills, but his will to win. The way he drove on the other players and how he wasn't afraid to give out to them if they weren't playing their best. It's something he tried to do when he was on the pitch, too.

'I'll give you 20 quid if you can do 300!' laughed his dad.

'Deal!' said Johnny. 'You're on!'

Johnny stayed out there for the whole afternoon. He didn't notice the hours passing or the tiredness creeping into his legs. The only thing he wanted was to keep practising and get his hands on the money. Just before dark, he called his dad back out.

'Right, let's do this!' he said, with determination on his face.

Go, Johnny, Go!

'Show me what you've got, son', smiled his dad.

'20 quid if I do 300?' asked Johnny, checking the fine print.

'A deal's a deal,' said his dad.

Off Johnny went. First he got 10, then 20, then 50. He was fully in control. He was at 100 now and counting. Right foot, left foot. A few on his knee. One or two headers. Now he was just showing off. His dad looked on proudly. Then he started to worry he would have to part with the cash. Now he was at 200, then 250. There was no stopping this lad when he put his mind to it. A few more flicks and tricks. He even threw in a back heel for good measure. He scooped up the ball to finish with a final flourish. A header. Then he trapped the ball on the back of his neck.

'I did it – 300,' he looked up at his dad with a grin. 'I believe you owe me 20 quid!'

'I believe I do', said his dad as he peeled open his wallet. 'Good man, Johnny. I knew

Will to win

you could do it.' He handed over the money and they shook hands.

'Pleasure doing business with you!' laughed Johnny. He was delighted.

When Johnny wasn't playing sport, he was watching it. The whole family were huge sports fans. He loved it when he was allowed stay up late to watch Manchester United in the Champions League. He would never forget Roy Keane's famous performance in the semi-final against Juventus.

Roy had scored the first goal but then got booked. This meant he would miss the final. Most players would have given up at this point, but not Roy. He got even better. In one of the greatest ever displays in the Champions League, Roy put his teammates before himself. He played like the Terminator.

Johnny jumped up from the couch. He punched the air when the third goal went in. United were on their way to the final. They went on to win the Cup, with one of the greatest comebacks ever. It was all thanks to

Go, Johnny, Go

Roy. Johnny learned so many lessons from watching him. Work hard. Encourage your teammates. Lead by example. Most important, he learned to never give up.

Johnny would sometimes watch big matches with his dad, like the 1997 Lions tour to South Africa. Johnny watched with wide eyes as the Lions beat the world champions in thrilling style. Everyone cheered on Ireland's Keith Wood as he crashed through the South Africans. It felt special. He loved the idea of the best of Ireland, England, Scotland and Wales coming together, putting their differences aside, to play for the Lions. He wondered if he would be good enough to wear that special red jersey one day.

Soon after, Johnny started secondary school. That's when rugby really took over.

Chapter 5

St Mary's

Johnny was so nervous on his first day at St Mary's. He was shy and quiet in class. That all changed once he got onto the field. No matter what the sport, he always came into his own. He soon made lots of friends. He would stay close to them for the rest of his life. St Mary's wasn't a big school, but it had a long history of rugby success. Rugby was everything there. It wasn't long until Johnny was eating, sleeping and breathing the game.

Johnny started to live like a real rugby player. He trained four times per week. He played two matches per week. He met teachers and coaches who would shape his future

Go, Johnny, Go!

career. They thought rugby was a great game to teach young boys about teamwork. How to win the right way and lose the right way. How to respect your opponents. St Mary's didn't have as many star players as some of the other schools they played against. They focused on team spirit instead. Johnny quickly learned how important it was to stick together.

He learned new skills. He started weight training and followed a special diet. Plenty of vegetables and lots of protein, like chicken and fish. He had to cut down on sweets and cakes too. Rugby can be a dangerous sport, so Johnny had to learn how to do things right. How to tackle, ruck and maul properly. Sport had always been Johnny's life, but this was better than he could have ever imagined. He was in heaven.

Johnny was always the first player on the training pitch and the last one to leave. He spent every minute he could with a ball in his hands. Even outside organised training, he would play matches at lunch break, getting his

St Mary's

uniform filthy. He'd come home wrecked and ready to eat everything around him. Johnny loved talking tactics, too. He started to study the playbook in great detail. He had a natural rugby brain. He could see things before others spotted them. The coaches already knew they had someone special on their hands. They had seen talented players before. They had also seen players who work hard. When talented players put in the hard work, that's when the magic happens. Johnny was one of them.

Johnny had an early taste of success in the under-13s Cup. He was soon making a name for himself across schoolboy rugby in Dublin.

'Have you heard about the young fella at Mary's? He has it all.'

'This Sexton lad is something else.'

'He's a flyer with silky skills. He's as tough as nails, too!'

Johnny moved quickly through the ranks. When he was 16, and still only in fourth year, he started playing for the St Mary's school senior Cup team. It was a huge honour. It

Go, Johnny, Go!

wasn't going to be easy. Most of the players he would face were already doing their Leaving Cert. Some of them would be two or three years older than him. Johnny was tall, but he hadn't filled out or bulked up yet. When many of his teammates were doing weights over the summer, Johnny preferred to spend his time playing golf or tennis. Now he wished he had worked on his strength a bit more. But he loved a challenge. There was no way he was turning down this chance.

St Mary's had a great season. They marched into the schools' Cup final. It was to be played at Lansdowne Road, the home of Irish rugby, on St Patrick's Day, 2002. Johnny was in dreamland.

It was a dirty day in Dublin, with driving rain and a wicked wind. Johnny was up early, already playing through the game in his mind. He was named on the bench, but he knew he would have a big role to play. He and his teammates had prepared like professionals all year. Now they were going to play like

St Mary's

professionals. Butterflies fluttered in his stomach on the bus journey to the game. Nearing the stadium, they could see all the fans already gathering. Blue flags for Mary's. Black and white for their opponents, Belvedere. The atmosphere was building.

They entered the tunnel and jumped off the bus. Johnny tried to play it cool but his heart was racing. This was really it. He was inside the dressing room in Lansdowne Road. Every Irish star had pulled on the green jersey here over the years.

St Mary's made a bright start. The first try came after just 7 minutes. Joey Connolly, Johnny's rival for the out-half slot, danced powerfully over the line.

'Yes!' Johnny jumped from the bench and punched the air. 'Nice one, Joey!'

The conditions made it difficult to get any decent play going. The pitch was cutting up and the ball was as slippery as a bar of soap. Belvedere ground their way back into the match. They soon narrowed the score to 7-6.

Go, Johnny, Go!

Belvo were getting stronger and Mary's were starting to tire. Johnny got the nod.

'Get ready, Johnny. You're going on,' his coach barked from the sideline.

Johnny's mind was spinning as he crossed the white line and stepped onto the Lansdowne Road turf for the first time.

'Breathe,' he told himself. He had just a few minutes to make his mark.

Belvedere were pushing hard for the winning score. Johnny knew he had to put in a big shift in defence. Standing firm, tackle after tackle. Then he got his chance in attack. Just 2 minutes after coming on, Mary's made some ground. They hit a ruck inside the Belvedere half, just within range of the posts. Johnny saw his chance. The drop goal was on.

Johnny dropped back into the pocket. It was a long way out. Right at the end of his range. He didn't even stop to think about how nervous he was. This was what all the training was for.

'Yes, Gibbo!' he roared to his scrum-half. The ball came quickly but the delivery was

St Mary's

slightly off. It was heading for his toes. Quick as a flash, Johnny fixed his stance. He stooped to collect the ball. The Belvo defence were rushing out to charge him down. There was no time to waste. In one movement he lifted the ball, dropped it and swung his right boot. The ball flew into the driving rain, towards the south terrace. The crowd of 11,000 watched in disbelief. They'd never seen a schoolboy take on such a kick before.

It whizzed straight down the middle, between the posts and over the bar.

Drop goal! Johnny Sexton wins it for Mary's!

Has there ever been a more dramatic kick in the history of school rugby?

Johnny didn't even celebrate. He jogged gently back to take his place in defence. There were a few minutes to go yet, but Belvedere couldn't come back again. Referee Alain Rolland finally blew the whistle. It was over. Mary's had won the Cup.

Go, Johnny, Go!

Johnny was mobbed by his teammates. Every schoolboy in the stand wanted to be in Johnny's shoes. His teachers, coaches and his parents were thrilled. It was just the fifth time St Mary's had won the Cup in 116 years. And they had Johnny to thank for it. A star in the making.

Chapter 6
Overlooked

Johnny played Senior Cup rugby for another couple of years at St Mary's. He even captained the team in his Leaving Cert year. But the drop goal on that St Patrick's Day final in 2002 would be as good as it got for him. No other moment came close. He was picked for the Leinster and Ireland schools' teams, but a couple of badly timed injuries meant he never quite got the chance to shine he wanted. His only focus was making the Leinster Academy.

The Leinster Academy was where you had to be if you wanted to make it as a professional rugby player. They hadn't been in touch with Johnny yet. He looked on with disappointment as his teammates were selected and given contracts. Johnny was overlooked. He was devastated.

For the last six years all he had ever thought about was being a rugby player. Now he had to think of something else. Johnny was clever and good at school. He thought that maybe he would like to study medicine. Dr Sexton had a nice ring to it! He studied hard for his Leaving Cert. He put the same focus and dedication to hitting the books as he did to hitting tackle bags. When the results came out, he was just short of the points he needed. Instead, he decided to study chemical engineering in UCD.

Johnny wasn't going to give up on his dream just yet, though. He was called up to senior level for the St Mary's club team to play in the All-Ireland league. He was a boy among men. The hits were fierce. He felt like he was playing against giants. They were only too happy to take a pop at the star of schools' rugby. Johnny needed to learn how to protect himself. He had to grow up fast.

Overlooked

Around this time, things were starting to get serious with his girlfriend, Laura, too. They had known each other since they were 12 years old. She was from just down the road and they had met at Rathgar Tennis Club. Johnny had spent most of his summers there when he was a boy. It was just out the back of his house. It was so close that his dad could call him home for dinner without leaving the garden. Johnny and Laura hit it off as soon as they met. They went out for a while and then went their separate ways. Now they were back together and going strong. Laura went to all his matches to support him. She was there so often she even knew the lineout calls. Johnny already knew she was the one he would spend the rest of his life with.

Johnny didn't like his course in college and soon realised chemical engineering wasn't for him. He was at a loss over what to do. He had done a few odd jobs about the place during his teenage years. He had worked in the bar at Bective for a while, washing glasses during

Go, Johnny, Go!

matches at Donnybrook Stadium. It was a great trick to get in to see the games for free and he got some pocket money for it, too. His mam ran a hair salon in Rathgar. He did plenty of shifts there, as well as in other shops around the village. But he thought maybe now was the time to get a real job.

Johnny started his new career at a building society called Friends First. He was kept busy answering the phones, and making tea and coffee. His dreams of playing for Leinster and Ireland were slowly slipping away. But he still had rugby. His mind was always looking ahead to the weekend, to the next St Mary's match in the All-Ireland league.

Johnny wasn't afraid to mix it with the grown-ups in the league. He was fast learning how to handle himself. He was already more skilful than most of them and now he was getting stronger week by week. He made himself heard in the dressing room, too. One day, he came into the clubhouse, put his bag down on an old wooden bench and started to get changed.

Overlooked

'Right,' he said, 'this is how we're going to play it today.'

The other players looked around in disbelief. **Who does this young fella think he is? Coming in here, telling us what to do!**

The more they listened, though, the more they realised he had something to say. It was clear their teenage out-half was a natural leader.

'You know what you're talking about, Sexto, I'll give you that,' laughed Coach Peter Smyth. He knew Johnny wouldn't be playing All-Ireland league for long. He was too good to be overlooked.

Away from working and training, Johnny spent his spare time relaxing, watching TV box sets or sport. He loved reading books, too, especially sports books. Sometimes he would even do the crossword in the newspapers. It was good for his concentration, which helped him to remember the play calls when he was on the pitch. After all, the out-half wasn't just the star player. He had to be the brains of the team, too.

Go, Johnny, Go!

Johnny waited and waited for the call from Leinster. But his phone never rang. Rather than give up, it made him more determined than ever to push on. He trained harder, practised more. In matches, he put his body on the line like never before. He learned how preparation during the week was key to performing in big games. He would take notes and study them before the weekend's match. He was a rugby nerd.

Finally, the break he was waiting for came. Like many things in life, it happened when he least expected it.

St Mary's were playing a league match against Dungannon at Templeville Road. Johnny didn't know it at the time, but the Ireland under-21 coach Mark McDermott was standing on the touchline. He had come to see a talented young out-half that everyone was talking about. But it wasn't Johnny Sexton. It was Dungannon's Gareth Steenson.

As luck would have it, Johnny played a stormer that day. He scored two tries and

Overlooked

kicked a load of points. He couldn't have planned it better. He was immediately called up to the Ireland under-21 squad for the World Cup in Scotland. They were up against Argentina, France and New Zealand. They were big, strong teams and the coach wanted men, not boys.

This was Johnny's big chance and he made the most of it. Soon after that, the call from Leinster came. They offered him a place at their academy. It didn't take Johnny long to accept. He had finally made it! It was everything he had ever dreamed of. All his sacrifice had paid off. But the hard work was only just beginning.

Chapter 7

Life at Leinster

Johnny was in awe on his first day in his new surroundings. There were rugby superstars everywhere. Gordon D'Arcy smashing a tackle bag. Brian O'Driscoll showing off his magic hands. Felipe Contepomi kicking goals for fun. The best in the world were all around him. It was the perfect place to learn. He was right where he wanted to be.

Johnny knew he was a good player. But these guys were on another level. He had to become more professional in every part of his life. Preparation, diet, training and effort. Some of the lads called him 'Coat-hanger' because of his slim build and narrow shoulders. He hit

Life at Leinster

the weights hard. He practised his squats, his jumps and his bench-presses. He got stronger by the day. But the gym was only a small part.

During training, Johnny watched how O'Driscoll moved the ball and opened space with his magic hands. He saw how D'Arcy controlled the defence and was always alive to danger. He noticed how Felipe ran the back line and kicked for touch. He started to prepare better for games. He wrote up his notes every day and studied them each Friday. He always cleaned his boots, washed his kit and packed his match-day bag the day before, so he wouldn't be running around in a panic on the morning of a game. They were small things, but they made a big difference. They were things all the best players in the world did.

Finally, Johnny was ready. After training one day, Leinster's coach Michael Cheika came over to him. Cheiks, as they called him, was a big, tough Australian. He could be quite scary at times.

'Johnny! A word,' he yelled.

Go, Johnny, Go!

'What have I done now?' thought Johnny to himself.

'Listen, mate,' said Cheiks. 'I've been watching you for a while. I think it's time to throw you in. Sink or swim.'

Johnny's mind was spinning. His moment had finally arrived. He was going to play his first match for Leinster. He thought his dream had died only a year before. Now it was more alive than ever.

'I won't let you down,' he stuttered. He could hardly believe what was about to happen.

On Friday night, 27 January 2006, Johnny made his first appearance in a Leinster shirt. Most people there wouldn't remember it. But for Johnny, it was the greatest moment of his life. Leinster were playing the Border Reivers from Scotland and Johnny started on the bench. He sat beside giant second-row Devin Toner, who was also making his first appearance. They both looked on as the Blues tore their opponents apart. It was a Felipe

Life at Leinster

Contepomi masterclass. The Argentinian out-half was a hero of the Donnybrook crowd. It was easy to see why. He scored a try and eight kicks in a one-sided game before he was finally called ashore.

'Let's go, Johnny,' shouted Cheiks. 'Follow that!'

Johnny was replacing the great Contepomi on one of his finest nights. He knew it wasn't a time to shine. He just wanted to survive for now. He had 15 minutes in the spotlight and he loved every second. The famous blue shirt of Leinster was finally on his back. It was a proud day for his mam and dad, Laura, and his brothers and sister. He had his first taste and now he wanted much more.

Johnny had to wait another 12 months for his first start, but it was worth the wait. Just a few days before Christmas, he was given the nod. It was to be a game against Leinster's biggest rivals, Munster, at Thomond Park in Limerick. Just up the road from Listowel, where his dad grew up. There would be no selection

Go, Johnny, Go!

boxes for Johnny that year. He spent Christmas Day training and getting ready for the biggest match of his life. The only thing he wanted from Santa was a win!

There was great joking with his Kerry relations in the run up to the game. His godfather, Billy, sent him a text. 'We hope you score loads of points and win Man of the Match. But Munster to win!'

Johnny's dad had no such divided loyalties. He was firmly behind Johnny.

'Munster by birth, Leinster by grace of God.'

In those days Munster were much better than Leinster. They were the European Champions and their team was full of legends like Axel Foley, Paul O'Connell, Donncha O'Callaghan and Ronan O'Gara. They won everything. It sickened Leinster that they couldn't come close to matching them. They were seen as the hard men of Irish rugby. The winners. Leinster were known as the losers who didn't like to get down and dirty. They

Life at Leinster

hated it. But the fact was they just weren't as good as Munster.

Thomond Park was the toughest place to go in rugby and Munster never lost there. Johnny was about to go into the lions' den. The bus journey to the grounds was a sea of red. The Munster fans were up for this match. 'Stand up and fight,' they sang.

Johnny took time to himself in the changing room. 'Play the game, not the occasion. Keep it simple. Go through the process,' he told himself.

It was hard to manage the nerves on a night like this. He looked around. He was in good company. Drico, D'Arcy and Shane 'Shaggy' Horgan were getting their game faces on.

'Let's go, Sexto,' shouted Drico, as he gave him a slap on the back.

Johnny just nodded. It wasn't a time for words.

They left the dressing room and squared up to Munster in the tunnel. Johnny looked

Go, Johnny, Go!

them up and down. Giants of the game. Ready for battle. Among them stood the one and only Ronan O'Gara, Johnny's hero. The one he watched running the show against Australia with his dad at Lansdowne Road just a couple of years before. Now they stood shoulder to shoulder. Equals. Johnny and ROG. Rival number 10s for Munster and Leinster. Johnny had to pinch himself.

Then he cleared his mind. It was time to play.

Five minutes in, Johnny landed his first shot on goal and Leinster were ahead. That settled the nerves.

'Nice one, Sexto!' called D'Arcy, as he jogged back to the halfway line. Johnny's first points for Leinster were in the bag.

It was a thrilling game. Munster crashed over for the first try. Minutes later Leinster hit back. Johnny was at the heart of a move that fed the ball to full back Girvan Dempsey.

Try!

Life at Leinster

Johnny kicked another penalty just before the break. Leinster were now ahead 11-10. This was going well.

But that was as good as it got for Leinster. Munster's forwards turned on the power in the second half. They strangled the life out of Leinster. ROG showed Johnny how it was done. He ran the show with a flawless exhibition of kicking, scoring 20 points with his boot.

Another one straight down the middle. He hardly ever misses!

Leinster had been thumped. It was hard to take. Even though he had played well, Johnny was very upset. He hated losing. A new rivalry had begun.

It was round one to ROG, but Johnny knew he'd be back for more. He wanted revenge.

Chapter 8
Setback

Despite his bright start, Johnny didn't kick on at Leinster like he expected. He started now and then, but would fall out of favour. It was annoying. It didn't help Johnny that the world-class Felipe Contepomi was his rival for the number 10 jersey. He was a Leinster legend. He also had more than 100 caps for Argentina. Johnny knew he couldn't complain, but he was impatient. He always wanted to be the best.

There was a big crop of talented youngsters all coming through at the same time. Players like Rob Kearney, Luke Fitzgerald, Devin Toner and Cian Healy. Johnny had played against some of them in school. It was hard for him

Setback

to watch as their careers took off and shot skywards like a rocket. Kearney and Fitzgerald were already flying. Everyone was talking about them as the next big stars of Irish rugby. Johnny was still kicking his heels, waiting for a chance.

Johnny got a chance at the start of the next season. With most of Leinster's star players at the World Cup in France, Johnny got a longer run in the team. Cheiks finally trusted him. He got off to a flyer against Edinburgh.

A try for Johnny Sexton! The future of Leinster rugby is in safe hands!

Then came Cardiff Blues.

Another try for Sexton! The St Mary's man does it again!

Next, he showed Scarlets the full force of his boot.

A huge kick! Sexton's feet are made of magic!

How did Johnny follow that? With another 23 points against Ulster and Glasgow! He was on fire by this stage.

Go, Johnny, Go!

This young lad has a hell of a future! Leinster are top of the table!

But once the World Cup stars returned, Johnny was back to the bench. It was hard to take. He started to get some offers to move on and he wondered if his future would be better elsewhere.

He thought about it long and hard. He spoke to his dad to get some advice. He would make some money and he would be starting games regularly. But in his heart, Johnny knew he only ever wanted to play for his hometown club. It was always about winning with Leinster and playing for Ireland. That was the dream. He reminded himself how lucky he was to be in the position he was in. His younger brother Mark was making a name for himself back in school at St Mary's, following in Johnny's footsteps. But Mark suffered a horrible leg break. It ruined his chance of a career in rugby. It was a wake-up call to Johnny. Everything he had could all be gone in a flash. So he decided to stick it out.

Setback

He decided to work even harder and wait for his chance.

Finally, an accident for a teammate was just the chance Johnny needed. D'Arcy broke his arm playing for Ireland in the Six Nations. The bone had smashed in seven places.

Owwwww!

It meant Leinster had to shuffle their pack. Felipe was moved to centre. It opened the number 10 slot for Johnny. He took the opportunity with both hands, skilfully guiding Leinster to win after win. He was motoring again.

The sweetest win of all came in April, when old rivals Munster came to the RDS. Leinster were unstoppable and Johnny played a starring role in a 21-12 win. He finished his performance with his speciality, a late drop kick.

Sexton drops back into the pocket. He wants the ball. He gets the ball. He swings his boot. And it's over! It's over!

A few weeks later, Leinster were crowned League champions. Johnny had played a huge

Go, Johnny, Go!

part. He had finally got his hands on some silverware. But the glory didn't last long.

That summer, Leinster signed Isa Nacewa. He was a star from New Zealand who played out-half. The news was hard for Johnny to take.

He met his old club coach at St Mary's, Peter Smyth, for a chat.

'You're looking a bit miserable, Johnny. Everything OK?' asked Peter.

'Yeah, all good. I've just lost a bit of confidence,' said Johnny. 'I need games, but I can't get into the Leinster team. It's hard going. It's not exactly how I imagined it.'

'You've still got all the talent, Johnny. Don't forget it. Listen, why don't you come back and play for Mary's for a while? It'll be good for you. Just have the craic with your mates.'

'Thanks, Peter. Sounds like a plan. Sure, what else would I be doing?' laughed Johnny.

So Johnny returned to the club. He got the games he needed, and he started to fall in love with the game again. He was playing with all his old friends, without pressure. His brother

Setback

Mark was in the team, too, making his way back to fitness from his leg break. It was just what Johnny needed.

Johnny simply played the game he loved. He didn't try to impress anyone. He realised he had been trying to copy Felipe and Isa. He had been trying to play their game, instead of focusing on what he was good at. He wasn't the next Contepomi or Nacewa. He was Johnny Sexton. The one and only.

After some fine performances for Mary's, Johnny got a call-up for the Ireland A team at the start of 2009. It was a huge honour to represent Ireland at the level just below the national team. The coach, Declan Kidney, showed faith in Johnny. That meant a lot to him. He had a very good night against Scotland at the RDS. He even scored a try. His whole family were there to watch. The performance gave him a huge lift and it turned his season around. It gave him a taste for more.

After the match, he got a phone call from Cheiks.

Go, Johnny, Go!

'Well played, Johnny. Great game,' he said. 'Listen, we want to give you a new contract at Leinster. How would you like to sign on for two more years? You're our future and we need you here.'

It was a short conversation. Johnny said yes straight away. It was just the vote of confidence he needed. Everything was looking good again. How quickly things can change. Johnny realised that in life your big break often comes just when you're on the point of giving up.

Chapter 9

Time to shine

It was the biggest match in club rugby anywhere in the world. The two biggest rivals in the game, Munster and Leinster, had been drawn together in the 2009 European Cup semi-final. There were 82,208 tickets sold for the historic match at Croke Park in Dublin. It was the only thing anyone could talk about. It was a rugby war. Family and friends divided. Neither side could bear the thought of losing.

It was a fine summer's day and the capital city was awash with colour. The blue of Leinster and the red of Munster. Johnny was a bag of nerves on the bus, as they travelled north towards the stadium. He had been

Go, Johnny, Go!

called up late to the squad after Rob Kearney strained his back. Isa moved to full back. Shaggy Horgan came in on the wing. This meant there was a spot for Johnny on the bench.

So here he was. On his way to Croke Park for the biggest game in Leinster's history.

The tunes were pumping on the bus, but Johnny was trying to keep his mind quiet and calm the butterflies in his stomach. The crowds got bigger as they passed along Pearse Street, on the way to the stadium. Thousands of people lined the streets. Johnny suddenly spotted a bunch of his friends from St Mary's. They were jumping up and down, waving Leinster flags and scarfs. Johnny roared laughing and waved back. How had he managed to spot them? Was it a good sign? Suddenly, his nerves disappeared.

Munster were strong favourites for the match. They were double European champions and had won their last 10 matches. They had already beaten Leinster twice this season.

Time to shine

The stadium was shaking long before kick-off. From deep inside the dressing room, the singing was loud and clear.

Leinster!
Munster!

Johnny had never felt anything like it. The team came in for a huddle. Drico spoke about all the times he had lost to Munster. All the heartbreak. All the near misses.

'It all ends today,' he said. 'They call us names. They don't respect us. But there's only one way to win respect. Out on the field. Today. Stick together. Stay together. Trust your teammates. We can do this. Don't give up!'

It was an inspirational speech. Johnny got a shiver down his spine.

'Come on, boys!' roared captain Leo Cullen.

The noise was deafening as they ran on to the field. A sea of blue and red, all mixed together. Both sets of players belted out the national anthem. It was a truly special occasion.

Munster knew it would be a tough match right from the first whistle. There wasn't an

Go, Johnny, Go!

inch of space. Players smashed and collided with all their might. Contepomi set the tone with an early charge at ROG. He landed a drop goal, before ROG levelled the scores again with a penalty. The first 25 minutes went by in a flash. It was a gripping contest. Nobody could take their eyes off it.

Then came the moment that would change the course of Johnny's life. With 26 minutes on the clock, Contepomi gathered the ball and set off on his trademark run. He switched direction from left to right, moving his weight from one side to the other. Suddenly, his knee buckled. He collapsed under the pressure. He could feel a shooting pain down the side of his leg.

Owwwww!

The doctor ran onto the pitch to check him out. It wasn't good. He had to come off. Cheiks looked across to the bench.

'Let's go, Johnny!' he shouted.

A shiver ran down Johnny's spine. This was it. It was time to shine. He was ready.

Time to shine

Johnny's first act was to line up a penalty. He was shaking with nerves. He had never felt an atmosphere like it before. He had never played in front of so many people. His knees were shaking. His heart was racing. He went through his routine. He took a deep breath and went for it.

It's a sweet strike from Sexton. Leinster are back in front!

The crowd roared. The kick had settled his nerves. He was ready to show the world what he could do. Minutes later, he set Leinster on the attack once more.

A long pass from Sexton. Here's O'Driscoll. He's brought in Nacewa. Now, can he feed D'Arcy? D'Arcy's nearly there. He's sliding on ...

A try for Leinster!

Johnny felt a surge through his body. D'Arcy had powered over the line and the crowd went wild. The noise was ear-splitting. Johnny's blood was pumping. The Munster players lay on the try line with their heads

Go, Johnny, Go!

in their hands. ROG was right there among them. Right at the start of the second half, Leinster came again. Another long pass from Sexton to O'Driscoll and Nacewa. Just like before. Then Horgan flicked it on to Fitzgerald. The flying winger showed his dancing feet and was quickly off on his way to the try line.

'Go on, Lukey,' screamed Johnny.

Try! Leinster are in control!

Munster were out on their feet. They couldn't live with Leinster's energy. The boys in blue had waited too long for this. They weren't going to let it slip today. The game was put to bed with yet another piece of Drico magic. He timed his run to perfection. He picked off a pass from ROG and ran almost the whole length of the pitch to score.

Brian O'Driscoll does it again. Game over!

Sexton slotted the conversion to wrap up an unbelievable 25-6 win. Leinster were on their way to the final. More important, they

Time to shine

had finally got the better of their big rivals, Munster.

'You're the man, Johnny!' roared Drico.

'You're not too bad yourself, Drico,' laughed Johnny, still taking in what had happened.

The Leinster players lifted Johnny into the air as the fans sang his name.

The final was played a few weeks later, against English giants Leicester Tigers, in Edinburgh in Scotland. Johnny was even more nervous than the last time, now that he would be starting. He couldn't stop thinking about the game. He couldn't sleep and he had to force himself to eat. He just wanted kick-off to come.

It was a huge task for Leinster. Their first ever European final. This was Leicester's fifth and they had all the experience of playing big matches. But Leinster and Johnny had worked too hard for this moment. They weren't going to let it slip.

Drico led the team talk in the dressing room. 'I've waited ten years for this. All you young guys: Johnny, Healy, Big Dev, Seán

Go, Johnny, Go!

O'Brien. This is only your first or second time. But take it from me. This chance doesn't come around too often. You have to make it count.'

Johnny was so pumped.

Once again, thousands of Leinster fans had travelled to cheer on their team. Johnny's family and Laura were in the crowd, crossing their fingers and toes that everything would be OK. On the pitch, Johnny stepped up to start the match. He looked around. He took a deep breath. His nerves suddenly disappeared.

Just minutes into the match, he showed the world just how ready he was. A poor defensive kick from Leicester landed in the arms of Gordon D'Arcy on the halfway line. Johnny gave a quick shout and D'Arcy popped the ball inside. Johnny, like he had done so many times before, took one look and went for his trademark long-range drop goal.

Sexton with a long, long drop goal. Leicester look nervous. They should look nervous!

Time to shine

But the Tigers hit back. They were 16-9 ahead by the second half. Leinster pushed forward again.

Crunch time in the match. Sexton to O'Driscoll. It's so tight!

Johnny made himself free for another pass and went again. He used every bit of energy he had. They were just inches short of the try line now. The ball popped out to Jamie Heaslip, who powered over.

Try!

Leinster were right back in it. There was nothing between them now. The scoreboard read 16-16.

Then, with ten minutes to go, Leinster got a penalty inside the Leicester half. There was only one thought in Johnny's mind. This was his shot. The kick to win the European Cup for Leinster, for the first time ever. No pressure!

He went through his routine, like he was practising in the park all on his own. He cleared his mind and made the crowd disappear.

'Make it just like any other kick,' he thought to himself.

Go, Johnny, Go!

Just a few months ago, Johnny had been down in the dumps. He thought his dream of playing for Leinster was over. Now he was standing over the biggest kick in Leinster's great history.

He looked at the posts, started his run-up and kicked like his life depended on it. But it was a horrible connection. He snatched it. He knew it was wrong the second he hit it. The ball went flying off to the right-hand side of the post. It was going wide. Johnny could feel his heart sink. With the eyes of the world watching, he thought he had missed. But suddenly, the ball started to move. It was bending back to the left, swirling through the air and towards the post. The roar of the Leinster fans erupted as it squeezed just inside and over the bar. It was so close, the ball scraped off some paint from the post.

It's there! Nobody was sure, certainly not the kicker!

'Lucky, lucky boy, Johnny!' shouted Drico.

Johnny puffed out his cheeks. He stuck out his tongue and laughed. Drico was right.

Time to shine

In the dying moments, every Leinster player gave everything they had left to defend their narrow lead. Johnny tackled himself to a standstill. It felt like the end would never come. Then he heard it. The sharp peep of the referee's final whistle. It was over. Leinster had won. Johnny had kicked the winning penalty in the European final.

'Yes, Johnny!' The players mobbed him. It was chaos on the field. The fans went wild in the stand. Johnny couldn't believe it.

Felipe was still on his crutches, hobbling around the celebrations. Johnny took a moment to join him.

'Well done, Johnny!' said Felipe, as he grabbed him in a tight hug.

'I learned everything from you, Felipe,' replied Johnny, with a smile.

'No, Johnny. You did it yourself. You're the future of Leinster now!' smiled the Argentinian ace.

They took to the stage. The players all linked arms. Big Leo Cullen put his hands on the shiny silver cup and lifted it high into the air.

'We are the champions, my friend!'

Johnny found Laura in the crowd and they shared a hug. It was an emotional moment for his parents, brothers and sister, and all his relations back in Kerry. They had seen Johnny through the hard times. Now he was the king of Europe. Today made it all worthwhile.

Chapter 10
Ireland

Now a European champion, and the Leinster number 10 jersey firmly on his back, it was time for Johnny to set his sights higher. He wanted to show what he could do in the green of Ireland.

Johnny's first chance came during the November internationals that year. Ireland were to play Fiji at the RDS. Everyone was saying this would be Johnny's big opportunity.

Earlier that week, coach Declan Kidney named the team. Johnny sat patiently in the dressing room listening to the names.

'Court, Flannery, Hayes, Cullen and O'Connell. Ferris, Leamy and Heaslip in the

Go, Johnny, Go!

back row. Eoin Reddan, scrum-half. Sexton at 10.'

There it was. The Ireland coach, reading out Johnny's name to start for the national team. It was another dream come true. He had to pinch himself.

He called his dad as soon as he could. 'Dad! I'm in!'

'Well done, son. I knew you would be. We're all so proud of you.' His dad sounded so happy on the phone.

'Thanks, Dad. I couldn't have done it without all your help,' said Johnny.

'Don't worry about that, Johnny,' said his dad. 'Now just go and show them what you can do!'

It was a horrible evening. Lashing rain with a howling wind. Johnny didn't care. He felt at home in the RDS, where he played for Leinster. The Ireland backs looked familiar. His Leinster teammates, D'Arcy, Drico, Shaggy and Kearney, were all starting behind him. Keith Earls was the only Munster man among them. There was

Ireland

a cracking atmosphere around the stadium. All of Johnny's family and friends were in the crowd. As the referee blew his whistle, Johnny decided to put on a show.

He struck a fine penalty 9 minutes in, giving Ireland the lead. At 18 minutes, Earls showed his pace for the opening try, and Johnny kicked over the conversion cleanly. Then came another perfect penalty on the stroke of half-time. Ireland were 13-3 ahead.

Johnny nailed another conversion just after the break, following a try by O'Driscoll. Then came another, after Earls scored his second. This time, Johnny had a huge kick from the touchline. After 68 minutes, Kearney slid over for yet another try in the corner. Johnny lined up another kick from out wide.

Right between the posts! This young man has the world at his feet!

But Ireland weren't finished yet. Shane Horgan touched down for the final try. Johnny added the icing on the cake. His final conversion made it seven kicks from seven.

Go, Johnny, Go!

A 100 per cent record. A perfect first start in green for Johnny.

'Outstanding, Johnny! Delighted for you!,' Earls said, as he patted him on the head.

'Dream debut, Johnny!' laughed Kearns, as he gave him a tight hug.

Johnny waved up at the stands, where Laura and his family were watching. He pumped his fists in the air. What a feeling! To make it even better, he was named Man of the Match.

Ireland's next match was to be against South Africa the following weekend at Croke Park. The big debate had started. Who should start at out-half? Johnny or ROG? Everyone had an opinion. Some thought ROG's experience should count. He was a legend. He had been there and done it time and again. He'd never let Ireland down. Others said Johnny should keep his place. He was the rising star. His time was now. He had a perfect game against Fiji. How could he be dropped?

Only one opinion really mattered. Coach Declan Kidney's. Just before the team

Ireland

announcement at the training camp, ROG came up to Johnny.

'Just a heads up, Johnny,' he said, 'you're starting on Saturday.'

Johnny couldn't believe it. It was the first time ROG had been dropped in six years.

'Deccie told me,' ROG continued. 'He told me I wasn't starting and there's no point keeping it a secret.'

ROG offered Johnny whatever help he needed in the build-up that week. Johnny was stunned. His biggest rival was offering to help him for the good of the team. This was what true sportspeople did. Johnny had huge respect for ROG. Later that evening, captain Paul O'Connell spoke to the squad.

'When we play for Munster, Leinster, Connacht or Ulster, we're the biggest rivals going,' he said.

The players hung on his every word. He was a legend and a fine speaker. Johnny loved just being in the same room as him.

Go, Johnny, Go!

'But in here, we're all the one. It's like playing against your brother. The last person you want to lose to is your brother. But then we all come together as a family. We play together for Ireland.'

It was a stirring speech. Johnny thought back to when he was young boy, knocking around with his own brothers on the patch of grass at Bective Rugby Club. Now he was playing for real, in the green of Ireland. And the World Champions were coming to town.

Johnny got a text from Contepomi the night before the game.

'Trust your instincts. Do the right thing for the team,' it said.

Johnny appreciated the support.

It was another cold November day in Dublin. Come kick-off, a heavy mist fell over Croke Park. It added to the magical atmosphere as Johnny took to the field. Fiji was one thing. The Springboks were something else. Declan Kidney had put his faith in Johnny. He knew he had to repay him.

Ireland

The tackles flew and the crowd booed. There wasn't an inch of space as the hits kept coming. The speed and power was like nothing Johnny had seen before. But he was holding his own. Then South Africa pounced. An early try, followed by a drop goal. Ireland were starting to slip. If the air was cold, then Johnny was even cooler. He had ice running through his veins when others were losing their temper. He clawed Ireland back into the match with his boot. He kicked two penalties so they were only four points behind at the break.

Ireland's defence put in a huge shift in the second half. South Africa began to run out of steam. Ireland could smell victory. Johnny calmly kicked another three penalties to grab a famous comeback win. The final score read 15-10. Johnny was the hero again. He had managed a mighty five kicks from five.

After the match, in the dressing room, as the adrenaline wore off, Johnny could feel a throbbing pain in his hand. The doctor had a look. Two broken bones.

Go, Johnny, Go!

Owwwww!

Johnny had broken his hand during the game. He hadn't even noticed. He played through the pain like a true warrior. Nothing could have dampened this special moment for him. A year that had started in despair was now ending in delight. From St Mary's and thoughts of quitting, Johnny had just kicked Ireland to a win over the world champions South Africa.

Johnny had one more job to do before the end of the year. He had some time off and travelled down to his dad's hometown of Listowel, in Kerry. He wanted to see his relations and reflect on a year that had changed his life. He walked into Keane's, where his godfather Billy was behind the bar. Johnny took something out from behind his back and put it on the counter.

'This is for you,' he said.

'What is it?' asked Billy.

'Open it and you'll find out,' laughed Johnny.

Ireland

Billy slowly unwrapped the present. It was his jersey from the match against Fiji. Framed, with something written underneath.

'To my godfather, Billy,' it read.

Billy looked up and smiled.

'I told you I'd do it,' Johnny smiled back. 'Now hang it on the wall like you promised.'

Chapter 11
Comeback king

A new era was dawning at Leinster. Some of the European Cup heroes, like Contepomi, Girvan Dempsey and Malcolm O'Kelly, had moved on. Coach Michael Cheika had stepped down, too. Word was spreading that Joe Schmidt would be the new head coach. Nobody knew much about him. He was a quiet New Zealander who had been working in France. But he made an instant impression when he arrived in Dublin.

Schmidt quickly laid down the law in training. Nobody was safe from his critical eye. Even the mighty Brian O'Driscoll. One afternoon in training, Drico dropped a ball. Schmidt was quick to jump in.

Comeback king

'Come on, Drico! Good players catch those!' he roared.

The rest of the players sat up and took notice. Johnny liked Joe straight away. They both hated losing. He knew they would get along.

Leinster found a new attacking groove under Joe. They blitzed everyone they came up against. They were playing at a higher level. Johnny was at the heart of it. He finally felt like he belonged. He was always snapping at players to perform better. Train harder. Work smarter. The players joked that he was Joe's general on the field.

Leinster had an almost perfect European season. They topped their pool with French giants Racing Métro and Clermont, and Saracens from England. Johnny was on fire. He scored a try and six kicks against Saracens. He touched down two more tries against Racing and kicked flawlessly throughout. He knocked over four from four as they got the better of Leicester in the

Go, Johnny, Go!

quarter-final. Then he had another perfect day in the semi-final against the mighty Toulouse. Drico and Heaslip scored the tries. Johnny kicked two conversions and six penalties from six. It was a great performance. Leinster were into another European final. Johnny was fast becoming known as one of the best players in the world.

Leinster were the hot favourites going into the final against Northampton, at the Millennium Stadium in Cardiff. Johnny got changed in the dressing room. Just before going out onto the pitch, he kneeled down to say a prayer. He prayed before every game. His nana and grandad back in Listowel had taught him the power of prayer when he was young. He did it since he was in school. It didn't mean he would win every game. He hoped it would help him from getting badly injured on the pitch. He always took a minute to himself before the team huddle. Today, he said a special prayer. His granddad John had died just a few months before. He thought of

Comeback king

him now. He prayed to him that everything would be OK.

Little did he know what would happen over the next two hours. The game kicked off. Suddenly, everything went wrong.

Northampton made the perfect start with a try after seven minutes. Leinster looked half asleep. They just couldn't get going. After half an hour, Northampton crashed over again. Then it went from bad to worse. England hooker Dylan Hartley scored again, right before half-time. Leinster were crushed. Northampton were 22-6 ahead. Johnny looked around in despair. They couldn't believe what was happening. Their European dream was already over. It was a shocking performance.

Johnny refused to give up. He ran to the dressing room like a man possessed. He encouraged his teammates to never give up.

'We see all the time that teams can come back. Like Liverpool a few years ago in the Champions League. They were 3-nil down to A. C. Milan but they came back. We can do

Go, Johnny, Go!

this!' he roared. 'Stuff like this happens. We have to believe. If we get the next score, they'll be rattled. Come on!'

It was a rousing speech. Johnny was stepping up to lead the team on and off the pitch. He was no longer the shy quiet boy who felt like he didn't belong. He filled his teammates' hearts with hope. Then he went onto the pitch and played the greatest half of rugby in the history of the European Cup.

The fire was still burning in Johnny's belly when he crossed the try-line just three minutes later.

Leinster throw everything at Northampton to get the first score of the second half!

Sexton! Try! They're back in the game!

Johnny squeezed the conversion off the inside of the post and over the bar. It was game on!

Leinster threw everything at Northampton. Johnny drove them on. He clapped his hands and shouted support. He grabbed the game by

Comeback king

the scruff of the neck. All thank to his sheer will to win.

Reddan to Sexton. Heaslip. Back to Sexton. Sexton looks for his second. He's going to get his second!

Try! Jonathan Sexton just refuses to lie down!

It was a remarkable ten minutes of rugby. Two tries from Johnny. But he wasn't finished yet. Far from it. Leinster's scrum was now on top and soon Johnny stood over a penalty.

Can Sexton drill this? Of course he can. The lead for Leinster! All the points from Johnny Sexton!

The Northampton players didn't know what was happening. They couldn't believe their eyes. One man had dragged Leinster from defeat to the edge of victory. Johnny Sexton. With 15 minutes left, Leinster had one hand on the trophy.

Try! Leinster drive over the line and into the history books! The greatest comeback of all time!

Go, Johnny, Go!

Johnny kicked one more for luck to seal a 33-22 win. Northampton didn't score in the second half. Johnny had landed 28 of Leinster's points.

The whistle blew and Johnny dropped to his knees. He had joined the greats. A double European Champion. Man of the Match in the final. A record comeback. A record individual points total. His granddad must have answered his prayer.

The Leinster fans were still in shock. Nobody in the stadium could believe what they had just seen.

'Johnny!' roared Seán O'Brien, as he ran across the pitch.

'What just happened?' laughed Drico. He could hardly believe they had won the game.

The players started dancing in a circle before they went up the steps to lift the cup.

'Nice speech at half-time, Johnny,' said Eoin Reddan, as he caught his breath.

'But what's all this stuff about Liverpool?' He joked. 'I thought you were a Man United fan!'

Comeback king

'True!' said Johnny. 'I'll never live that one down!'

The players did a lap of honour, singing and dancing with the Leinster fans. Johnny held the cup in his hands and looked to the sky. He remembered his family back home in Listowel. He looked back down and kissed the cup.

'That's for you, Granddad.'

Chapter 12
Johnny v ROG

Everything was going perfectly with Leinster. But when it came to playing for Ireland, it was a different story. Even though he was the hero against Fiji and South Africa, Johnny was dropped for the start of the Six Nations. It was hard to take. ROG had been a great servant to Irish rugby. He wasn't going to take losing his place easily. The battle for the number 10 shirt was back on.

Fresh blood or experience? Better defence or attacking flair? Drop goals or penalty kicks? Leinster or Munster?

Johnny Sexton or Ronan O'Gara?

It was the question on everyone's lips. The whole country had an opinion. The Leinster

Johnny v ROG

fans wanted Johnny. The Munster fans backed ROG. Everyone else picked a side. It was all over the newspapers and on TV. They both wanted to be number one. They were born winners. Fierce competitors. Neither wanted to give the other an inch. They were two of Ireland's best players but there was only room for one of them in the team.

The battle was taking its toll on Johnny.

ROG started the first two games of the tournament against Italy and France. Ireland played badly in Paris and lost to France. Johnny was back in for the next game against England.

It was his Six Nations debut. More pressure on his shoulders again. Another chance to show his worth. But he needn't have worried. It was another memorable day. Ireland won out on 20 points to 16.

Tommy Bowe!

The Ulster winger had scored two tries and Johnny kicked a conversion. Wins over England at Twickenham don't come often, so they had a big celebration. Johnny kept his place for a

Go, Johnny, Go!

win over Wales, as well as the final clash with Scotland at Croke Park to decide the Triple Crown. Just seven minutes in, he showed a burst of pace to set O'Driscoll free.

Try!

But Johnny's boot let him down. He missed a kick either side of half time and was replaced by ROG with half an hour to go. He was disgusted. Ireland lost in the end. It was a miserable day all round.

Johnny felt like two different people. The Johnny who played for Leinster and the Johnny who played for Ireland. At Leinster, he was the main man. He led by example, encouraged the players and drove standards. With Ireland, he went into his shell a bit more. He didn't really feel like himself.

One day, Drico called him over after training. 'Johnny, we need you to step up. We need you to drive us on like you do at Leinster,' he said.

'I can't, Drico. How can I? I don't even know if I'll be starting each week. I can't lead if I'm not in the team,' Johnny explained.

Johnny v ROG

ROG could see Johnny was ambitious and was coming after his place. He wasn't going to make life easy for him.

Both Johnny and ROG kept improving their skills to outshine the other guy. It was good news for Ireland.

It continued like that for another year. Johnny would play a few matches, then ROG would be back in. Neither player liked it, but they had to live with it. The coach's decision was final.

By 2011, Johnny started the Six Nations as the man in charge of the jersey once more. They survived a big scare in Rome, finally beating Italy by two points. Johnny knew he was under pressure. But his kicking touch left him altogether in Paris. It was a horrible feeling. He just couldn't seem to get it right.

'Why does it always happen to me playing for Ireland?' thought Johnny.

He wasn't surprised when ROG was back in for the next matches against Scotland and

Go, Johnny, Go!

Wales. ROG scored a try and kicked three from three against the Scots. Johnny was sick looking on from the sideline. ROG nailed all his kicks against Wales too. But his overall performance wasn't great. So Johnny was put back in on the starting team for a home clash against England. He knew it was time to bring his Leinster form to the green shirt of Ireland.

Ireland were out of the running for the Six Nations. England were going for a Grand Slam. Ireland were determined to stop them. Thousands of English fans travelled over to Dublin for the match. They were hoping it would be a big day to celebrate. But Ireland, and especially Johnny, had other ideas.

Johnny brought his shooting boots and fired three perfect penalties in a row. After 22 minutes, Ireland were 9-0 up and everyone was in shock.

Never in doubt the moment it left his boot!

Johnny tapped a quick penalty to set Ireland on the attack.

Johnny v ROG

Advantage to Ireland. Will Sexton take it quickly? He will, you know. Is it the right decision?

Try! Tommy Bowe! England have nodded off. Brilliant confidence by Sexton.

Johnny was pulling all the strings now. Ireland were 17-3 up at half time and it was about to get even better. O'Driscoll crashed over to become the record try-scorer in the history of the Six Nations.

'Drico, you legend!' shouted Johnny as he touched down.

Johnny took a deep breath and kicked another perfect one straight between the posts.

On its way from Sexton. It's one of those days when everything goes right!

Nobody saw Ireland's performance coming, least of all Johnny. They had stopped England winning the Grand Slam. Everyone was dancing in the stands as darkness fell over Dublin. Johnny was named Man of the Match. Finally, he felt like he belonged in the green shirt.

Chapter 13
World Cup

The win over England set Ireland up nicely for the World Cup in New Zealand later that year. Johnny still couldn't believe how far he had come. It was only two years since he thought his Leinster career was over. Now he was on a flight down under to start the World Cup as Ireland's star out-half. He was in great form on and off the pitch.

After a short break over the summer, Johnny returned to the Ireland training camp. He was still on a high after Leinster's amazing comeback in the European Cup final. He was playing some of the best rugby of his career. Even the long flight to New Zealand couldn't

World Cup

get his spirits down. It's one of the longest flights in the world and it takes almost a full day to get there. Johnny and his teammates had to make sure to keep stretching their muscles. They had to drink plenty of water and get as much rest as possible. Even though it was almost the end of summer in Ireland, it was winter in New Zealand. Everything seemed upside down on the other side of the world.

Ireland's first match was against the USA, on a wet day in Taranaki. It should have been an easy match, but it wasn't. Johnny started the match. ROG was on the bench. Ireland's play was sloppy. They made lots of mistakes. Johnny missed two early penalties, which didn't help.

'Come on, boys!' roared Johnny. 'Keep the heads up!'

Just before half-time, Tommy Bowe eased their nerves. Johnny set him free with a perfect pass.

Try!

Johnny still wasn't happy. His kicking was totally off. He was worried. He missed another

Go, Johnny, Go!

kick and Coach Kidney had seen enough. Johnny was pulled off early in the second half and replaced by ROG. Nightmare.

Ireland went on to win 22-10. A win is a win. But Johnny was disgusted with himself. Of all the days to lose his kicking touch.

Next up was a crunch clash against Australia. They were one of the best teams in the world. They had just beaten New Zealand and South Africa to win the Tri Nations. This was Ireland's biggest match of the pool stages. They had to win. Johnny sat nervously as Kidney named the starting team.

'No. 10, Sexton,' he barked.

'Phew,' thought Johnny.

What a relief. Johnny had kept his place. Just about. There was no room for any more mistakes or bad days. He had to play the game of his life.

Johnny felt the butterflies rumbling in his tummy on the team bus. It was a Saturday night kick-off, under floodlights at the famous Eden Park stadium. It was known as the House

World Cup

of Pain, because the All Blacks almost never lost there and opposing teams were often badly beaten. The atmosphere was electric. Even though it was 20,000 kilometres from Ireland, it felt like a home match. The stadium was full of Irish fans. They were in full voice. At the time, things were very hard for people in Ireland. People didn't have much money to spend. There were no jobs and life was tough. Lots of young Irish people had moved to Australia and New Zealand to find work. Now they had come to the stadium to cheer on Ireland. To give them a taste of home. The players knew this was a special occasion. It was more than just a game. They had to win for the fans.

Johnny missed an early penalty.

'Oh no,' he thought, as soon as he hit it. 'Not again.'

Thankfully, he kicked a perfect one just a few minutes later. Then he spotted a chance for a trademark drop goal.

'Redser!' Johnny screamed to Eoin Reddan.

Go, Johnny, Go!

The scrum-half dug the ball out from the back of a ruck. He spun a fizzing pass straight to Johnny, who thumped it low and hard, right between the posts.

Drop goal from Sexton!

It was 6-6 at half time. Right in the balance.

Ireland raised their game in the second half. Seán O'Brien was having the game of his life.

'Good man, Seánie.' Johnny patted him on the back, encouraging the big forward after he won Ireland a penalty.

Johnny lined it up. He had never felt pressure like it. He knew if he missed, ROG would be waiting in the wings.

'Trust the process,' he said to himself. He went through his familiar routine. He nailed it.

It's a perfect kick. Ireland are back in front!

Johnny had another chance to stretch the lead a few minutes later. It was a tougher kick. Further out to the touchline. He went through his routine.

He smacked it. The contact felt good. He was happy. It flew through the New Zealand

World Cup

night sky. Everyone in the stadium held their breath. It looked good the whole way. Then, at the last second, it turned slightly and came off the inside of the post.

'Just my luck,' thought Johnny. That miss was his last kick of the game. He was replaced by ROG, who kicked two from two to help Ireland win the game. It was one of the biggest shocks of the World Cup. The Irish fans went wild. The players hugged and celebrated. Even though he had played a big part, Johnny didn't feel like joining in. ROG was the hero of the day. That was hard to take.

That's the life of a kicker. Score and you're the hero. Miss and it's all your fault. Johnny had lived with the pressure all his life. It never got easier.

ROG was back in the starting team for the big win over Russia. He kicked seven out of eight. Then he demolished Italy with another great kicking display, this time six out of seven. He had found his shooting boots just as Johnny lost his. Johnny could only watch on from the bench.

Go, Johnny, Go!

Ireland's World Cup journey came down to a clash with Wales in the quarter-final. Ireland had never got past this stage at a World Cup before. But they had never had as good a chance as this time. They had beaten Wales a lot in recent times. They were confident of success. But nothing went to plan.

Johnny was on the bench again, but it made little difference. They were completely outplayed by the Welsh. It was a day to forget. A try by Keith Earls gave them a little hope early in the second half. But Wales won out comfortably. The final score was 22-10.

Johnny came on for the last 20 minutes. By then, he wasn't able to help much. Their World Cup journey was over. After all their early promise, Ireland had crashed out of the quarter-finals again. Johnny's World Cup dream had turned into a nightmare. He wondered if his Ireland career would ever match his glory days with Leinster.

Johnny was never in good form when he lost a match. This was even worse. He had

World Cup

been working towards the World Cup for two years. Now it had all crumbled to dust. He beat himself up over it. Any kicker can lose their touch every now and again. For it to happen at a World Cup, though, was hard to take.

He didn't stay grumpy for long. He decided to have a hard look at himself and his game. Was it his fault? Had he stopped working as hard as before? Had he taken his foot off the gas?

Johnny knew he had to learn from his mistakes and move on. Work harder. Re-invent his kicking technique. Improve again.

He had been here before. At school, at St Mary's, and with Leinster. Now he had to do it with Ireland. The setbacks always make you stronger.

Chapter 14
Back in blue

After the World Cup, Johnny went for a trip back down to Listowel to visit his Nana Breda. It was great to get away from everything and spend time with his family. He loved getting spoiled by his nana. He could go for walks on the beach, or for a game of golf in Ballybunion. It was the perfect way to clear his head. He still had to put up with some slagging from his uncles.

'It would've been grand if you'd just played for Munster, Johnny!' they laughed.

Before long, his holiday was over and Johnny was back in the blue of Leinster once more. They got into their rhythm quickly.

Back in blue

Once again, they moved up a gear under Joe Schmidt. They were winning match after match with ease. Leinster and Johnny were poetry in motion that season.

Johnny started as he meant to go on. He kicked six penalties, a drop goal and a conversion, as they put 36 points on Edinburgh.

Sexton's boot is heating up!

Then came another grudge match against Munster. Following the World Cup, everyone was talking about Johnny and ROG. The Aviva Stadium was packed with 48,000 fans. They were looking for a clash and it didn't disappoint. The two out-halves went blow for blow in a gripping defensive contest. Johnny eventually came out on top. He kicked seven penalties from seven as Leinster won 24-19.

Flawless Sexton shows ROG how it's done!

Leinster began their European journey with an important draw on the road in Montpellier. Johnny pulled the strings and kicked the points.

Go, Johnny, Go!

Sexton magnifique!

Soon Glasgow were gobbled up. Then they soaked Bath. Not once, but twice. Johnny kicked all 18 points in the first match. He added a try for good luck in the second game. Leinster won out 52-27.

'What a try, Johnny! You're on fire!' laughed Kearns, as they celebrated his try.

Leinster saw off Ulster and Connacht over Christmas and then crashed past Cardiff with a 23-19 win.

Johnny, the man. He's playing on a different planet!

It was down to the business end of the season now. Cardiff were their opponents again in the European Cup quarter-final. Leinster showed little mercy. Nacewa, Kearney and O'Driscoll all scored tries, helping the team to a 34-3 win. Johnny was fantastic. He showed his full range of tricks and flicks. He faked a dummy to set up Nacewa's try. He even threw in a no-look pass in the second half.

Back in blue

Sexton's just showing off now!

On top of all that he kicked another six right between the posts. The World Cup was long forgotten now!

French giants Clermont were Leinster's opposition in the semi-final. It was a bruising battle, but Johnny and his teammates pulled through once again. There was just no stopping them. This time, Cian Healy did the damage.

Try for Leinster!

Johnny added the conversion. Leinster won out by 19-15. They were off to another European final.

Before that, they travelled back down to Thomond Park. Their old enemies, Munster, lay in wait. It was a battle of the boots again. Every time Johnny kicked one over, ROG got one back. Leinster pulled ahead in the second half. There was no stopping the boys in blue this season.

'Two wins over Munster in the same season. That doesn't happen too often!' joked Johnny.

Go, Johnny, Go!

He was going to enjoy rubbing that in with his uncles from Kerry.

Johnny loved his new role at the heart of the team. He was a leading voice in the dressing room. He called plays on the field. He kept everyone on their toes off the pitch, too. He felt it was important to speak his mind, especially in training. If something wasn't working, he would say it. If he thought a teammate wasn't working hard enough, he had no problem telling them. Sometimes it got him in trouble. But that's what made him who he was. He blamed it on the Munster blood.

The perfect season ended with a perfect performance against Ulster in the final at Twickenham Stadium in London. An all-Irish clash at the home of English rugby. More than 80,000 fans made the journey across the Irish Sea for the game. Leinster put on a show.

Right from the start, they were in complete control. First-half tries from Seán O'Brien and Cian Healy had them well on their way. The magician O'Driscoll was calling the shots. Johnny was driving everything from behind the

Back in blue

scrum. He fired three conversions and three penalties, bringing his total to 15 points. Ulster were simply blown away. The final score was 42-14.

Leinster are the kings of Europe once more. The first team for ten years to win back-to-back European Cups!

Johnny lifted the cup for the third time in four years. He looked with pride at the medal around his neck. It was a sweet feeling after his World Cup disappointment just eight months before.

The players danced and sang long into the night in London. Johnny felt like he was on top of the world. He was with his family and friends and had just won the European Cup with his boyhood team. The only one he ever wanted to play for. He didn't know it at the time, but that would be his happiest moment in a Leinster shirt for quite some time.

Chapter 15
Leaving Leinster

Johnny had been in talks with Irish Rugby about a new contract for some time. He wasn't happy with the offer he got. He wasn't happy at all. He felt they weren't paying him what he was worth. He decided to look at other clubs to see if he could get a better deal. It wasn't so much about the money, but respect. He felt he should be rewarded for all the improvements he had made over the past four years. He was Ireland's starting out-half, a three-time European champion. He was rated as one of the best players in the world.

Johnny's agent told him there was plenty of interest in him and he soon got an offer. The

Leaving Leinster

Racing Métro team, based in Paris in France, wanted to sign Johnny. They wanted to build their team around him and make him the star. They were happy to pay him plenty of cash. It was more money than Johnny had ever dreamed of. It would set him up for life. He didn't really want to go. He hoped that Irish Rugby would match the offer. He wanted to stay at home with his friends and family in Dublin.

Soon news of Johnny's move to France was out. His teammates were quick to poke fun at him. One day, they left a French flag beside his gear bag in the dressing room.

'*Passez le ketchup*, Johnny!' they would joke at the dinner table.

The lads would start singing the French national anthem whenever Johnny walked by. It was all good-natured craic. But Johnny was deadly serious. If Irish Rugby didn't come back with a better offer, then he would leave.

He thought long and hard about it. He spoke to his mam and dad, his brothers and

Go, Johnny, Go!

sister. Mostly he chatted to Laura. It would be a big move for Johnny, but it would be even bigger for Laura. She was a teacher. She would have to give up her job for a few years to live in France. It was a hard decision. He just hoped he would get a better offer to stay in Ireland. But the longer he waited, the less likely it seemed.

With all this going on in the background, Johnny went about his business of playing rugby. Things weren't clicking on the field quite like last year. Leinster had been doing OK in the league and had some good wins. But they really struggled when it came to the European Cup. They were ranked as the number one team but lost twice to French team Clermont in the pool stages and surprisingly crashed out in early January. To make matters worse, it was Munster who went through instead of them. After all their success in previous years it was so disappointing for their European Cup run to end so early in the year.

Leaving Leinster

Johnny and his teammates didn't have much time to feel sorry for themselves. They were straight into Ireland camp for the Six Nations. It comes around quickly every year.

Ireland made the perfect start with a big win away to Wales in Cardiff. The game will always be remembered as a great display of skill from Simon Zebo. He flicked up the ball off his boot and went charging towards the try line.

What an outrageous piece of footwork from Zebo!

Johnny had a good day out too. He kicked six from six. Ireland were up and running. Everything looked good.

But things fell apart quickly in the next game, against England. Johnny started the match but lasted just half an hour. He was running at full tilt when suddenly ...

Owwwww!

Johnny felt a shooting pain up the back of his leg. He collapsed onto the Twickenham turf, his head in his hands. His hamstring was gone.

Go, Johnny, Go!

'It's not good, Johnny,' said the doctor. 'A grade-two tear. You'll be out for four to six weeks.'

'Nightmare,' was all Johnny could say.

It was the first time it had ever happened. His first major injury.

Worse still, Ireland lost the match 12-6. Their Grand Slam hopes were gone. Johnny's Six Nations was over before it began.

Without him, Ireland's performances went from bad to worse. Johnny was going mad as he watched the rest of the tournament on TV from the comfort of his couch. He wasn't a good spectator. It was a total disaster. Ireland even lost to Italy. They finished second last in the table.

Things weren't going any better for Johnny off the field either. Irish Rugby came back with a final contract offer. It wasn't near what he was looking for. It was time to make up his mind. Take the offer or take this huge chance?

Once more he talked it over with his family and Laura. He even rang Joe Schmidt, hoping

Leaving Leinster

he would be able to get Johnny a better deal. It all came to nothing.

After weeks of thinking about it, Johnny finally decided to move to France. It was a whole new world. He flew to Paris for talks and to look around his new city. The sights, sounds and smells were all so different. The training ground was spectacular. They had everything he would ever need. He went house hunting with Laura. They first looked at apartments in the city. Then they decided to live in an old farmhouse in the countryside. It was perfect. They were both so excited about their new adventure in France.

Johnny had a medical at the club where they checked to make sure everything was OK. Then he signed his new contract.

'This is it,' he whispered to Laura. 'No going back now!'

He was so excited about the move, but he was heartbroken too. How would he tell his teammates? They had been through everything together. They were his best friends. Despite

Go, Johnny, Go!

all the joking, they never really thought he was going to leave.

Johnny was training on the morning the news broke that he was moving to France. After kicking practice, he turned on his phone to a stream of texts.

'Is it true?'

'I'm so shocked.'

'Can't believe it!'

It was only then that Johnny fully realised what was happening. This was it. He locked himself away in his bedroom and he cried to himself on his bed.

Once his injury healed, Johnny still had to finish out the season with Leinster. They had fallen below their usual standard, but they still had two finals to fight. The European Challenge Cup final against Stade Français and the league final against Ulster a week later. Johnny was determined to go out on a high.

The Challenge Cup final went exactly to plan. Leinster soaked up all the Stade Français pressure and then hit them on the attack. Ian Madigan, Seán Cronin, Rob Kearney and Cian

Leaving Leinster

Healy all scored great tries and helped them to a 34-13 win. Johnny kicked 14 points. It was an emotional day in front of his home fans at the RDS. He went up to lift the cup alongside Isa Nacewa. They were both leaving at the end of the season. It was bittersweet for Johnny. Joy at winning, but sadness at leaving all of it behind.

The league final against Ulster came a week later, again at the RDS. It was to be Johnny's last game in the blue of Leinster before he headed for France. He didn't even think about losing. It took just three minutes for Shane Jennings to settle Leinster's nerves.

Try!

Ulster gave it their all, but Leinster always looked like the winners. Johnny kicked another 14 points. Jamie Heaslip finished off their 24-18 win with a late try.

Leinster are the champions!

There was so much going through Johnny's head when the final whistle blew. Regret, frustration, anger and love. He had

Go, Johnny, Go!

delivered two trophies in two weeks. He led his teammates on a lap of honour. The Leinster fans waved him off in style. It was the perfect send-off.

In the dressing room, Johnny worked up the courage to say a few words.

'I never thought this was going to happen. I'm really going to miss you,' he said with emotion in his voice. 'This team has been everything to me for the last seven years. I'm sure some of you will be glad to see the back of me. At least training will be quieter next year! But listen, I've a great adventure ahead of me. I'm going to give it all for my new team.'

'Three cheers for Johnny!' roared Reddan.

'Hip, hip, hooray!' they all shouted.

As Johnny left the RDS for the last time as a player, a supporter caught his eye and shouted, 'See you in two years, Johnny!'

Chapter 16

Lions

It was all happening for Johnny. He had just finished with Leinster, but before his big move to France, he had to squeeze in a Lions tour to Australia. It was the last remaining goal on Johnny's list since he was a boy. He always loved the idea of the Lions. The stars of Ireland, England, Scotland and Wales coming together to take on the best of the southern hemisphere. This time, the Aussies in a three-test series.

Johnny had been waiting all season for the call up. He was worried when he got injured during the Six Nations that it mightn't happen. He was relieved when he was finally picked

Go, Johnny, Go!

for the tour, along with his Ireland teammates Cian Healy, Paul O'Connell, Seán O'Brien, Jamie Heaslip, Brian O'Driscoll, Rob Kearney, Conor Murray and Tommy Bowe. It was the trip of a lifetime. A chance for Johnny to show he truly was one of the best players in the world.

Johnny showed enough form in the warm-up matches to be picked in the starting team for their first test in Brisbane. The match wasn't until late in the evening. He had a lot of time to kill that day. He hated waiting so long for kick-off. He had a late breakfast and went back to bed for a while to watch some TV.

When they finally arrived at the stadium, Johnny couldn't believe what he was seeing. Irish, English, Welsh and Scots all mixed together.

'Lions! Lions! Lions!' they roared.

The stadium was electric. The noise made it impossible for the players to hear each other on the pitch. The Aussies were up for this.

It took just 12 minutes for Australia to get their opening try. Their dangerous scrum-half

Lions

Will Genia tapped a quick penalty. He chipped the ball right over to Israel Folau, the flying winger making his first test start. There was no catching him.

Try!

The Lions were soon back on form, thanks to a stunning solo try from Welsh winger George North. But before half-time, Folau was in again. He stepped inside Johnny and they raced to the try line. Johnny was furious he let him past. But he made up for it shortly after. He fired a perfect pass to Alex Cuthbert, who powered over. The Lions were in front again.

What a cracker of a test match!

Australia came back again. With just a minute to go, the Lions' lead was down to two, 23-21. There was still time for more drama. The referee gave the home side a penalty. Kurtley Beale stepped up to take it. One kick to win the match. It was a long way out. Johnny fancied him to make it. He started his run-up. Just as he was about to strike the ball, he slipped.

Go, Johnny, Go!

Oh no! Beale has lost his footing. He's missed the kick. The Lions have won!

Johnny couldn't believe it. How lucky could they be? He'd never seen a slip like that. As a kicker himself, he felt sorry for Beale. But he was delighted the Lions had won. He was too tired to celebrate afterwards. He sat in the team room with Drico and Paul O'Connell. They shared a McDonald's and watched the match again on TV. He couldn't have been happier.

The second test was just as exciting and intense. This time, Australia won by a single point, 16-15. There was nothing between them. The series all came down to a third and final test in Sydney, at the start of July.

There was a huge shock when the team was named early in the week. Word had been circling and Kearns finally broke the news to Johnny.

'Did you hear about the team?' he asked.

'Just rumours. Jamie's gone?' Johnny replied.

'No, Drico. He's left him out.'

Lions

Johnny was speechless.

Brian O'Driscoll had been dropped for the first time since he was a schoolboy. One of the greatest players of all time. A Lions, Ireland and Leinster legend. Now he had been left out of the series decider, for what would have been his last act in a Lions jersey. It was heartbreaking. Johnny couldn't believe it. Everybody in Ireland went crazy. They thought Drico had been badly treated because the coach was Welsh. Johnny got a text from his brother Jerry to say it was the lead story back home on the news.

Johnny went to see Drico to say sorry and wish him well. He took it as well as he could. But things move quickly in professional sport. Johnny was starting the match. He had to be selfish and get his own mind on the game.

After the World Cup, winning a Lions series is the ultimate achievement for a rugby player. They only come around every four years. Few players even get a chance to make the team. Johnny knew they couldn't let this one slip. Any

Go, Johnny, Go!

kind of win would do today. The Lions were like men possessed as they entered the field in Sydney. The crowd of 82,000 was deafening once again.

Johnny launched the ball high into the air to get the game under way. It was the start of a thunderous move from the Lions that finished with a try after just one minute. Prop Corbisiero burst over the line. It was a fierce battle after that. Tight and tense. Just like the first two tests. It was right in the balance in the second half, just six points between them, when Johnny showed his genius.

Murray spun a pass out from the base of a ruck right into Johnny's hands. He showed a burst of speed. He took the ball to the line, before feeding Bowe, who popped it on to Davies. Davies slipped a tackle. He got his hands free and passed to the onrushing Halfpenny, who had sped forward from full back. Johnny kept his run going. He was suddenly free on the inside. He screamed for the ball. His eyes lit up.

Lions

Halfpenny dummies and there's Sexton. Jonathan Sexton! Brilliant try for the British and Irish Lions!

'Yeah!' Johnny let out a huge roar. He pumped his arms in the air.

'Johnny!' shouted Conor Murray. He was the first player over to congratulate him.

The Lions grabbed two more tries and won the match in style. The final score, 41-16. A hammering. It was a first series win for the Lions in 16 years. The players went mad on the pitch afterwards. It was one of the greatest nights of Johnny's life. He gave Drico the biggest hug. His Leinster and Ireland teammate, who would have loved to have been with him on the pitch.

'We did it for you, Drico!' said Johnny.

Amid all the madness in the dressing room, Johnny found the time to call home.

His mam was full of emotion. 'I'm just glad you didn't get hurt. That's the main thing,' she said. 'We're all just so proud of you. We were shouting and roaring, kissing and hugging. It's unbelievable!'

Go, Johnny, Go!

Johnny was on a high. He sang a song on the bus on the way to the team reception but was drowned out by the other players booing.

'Get off the stage!'

Johnny had no time to rest when he arrived home. Just a week later, he married his childhood sweetheart, Laura, at Adare Manor, just down the road from his dad's home town, Listowel. His brother Mark was best man. His other brother Jerry was groomsman, along with his cousin, Roy. All his teammates were there, including Drico and Kearns. ROG was there, too. Their rivalry was over. Now they were now great friends. Johnny's nana Brenda was also there. She was in her 80s now. She was so happy to see the little boy who used to kick a ball out the back of her house all grown up and marrying the love of his life.

Rugby was important for Johnny. But family always came first.

Johnny and Laura kissed at the altar to huge cheers. They danced the night away with

Lions

all their friends and relations. Then it was time to pack their bags for France.

Chapter 17
France

Johnny knew his life in France would be very different. But this was just weird. His new teammates at Racing Métro gave him a goldfish to mind on his first day. Then he was asked to eat it. He thought they were joking but they were serious. Johnny wasn't sure what to do. He didn't want to fail his first challenge. Thankfully, the club doctor stepped in to his rescue and told him not to eat it. His teammates burst out laughing.

'Bonjour à Paris, Johnny!' they said. 'Welcome to Paris.'

Johnny threw himself into life in Paris. He worked hard on and off the pitch. He

France

learned the language and got to know his new teammates. He and Laura lived near the training ground in a quiet area outside the city. He loved visiting local places to shop, eat or have a coffee. The big city was just 10 or 15 minutes away on the train if he wanted to see the Eiffel Tower or the sights of Paris. He listened to language lessons in his car driving to and from training. It was still a struggle, though. In one of his early games, he was calling a play as the ball came out.

'Paree!' he roared. It was the codename for a pre-planned move called Paris. He teammates couldn't understand what he saying. They thought he said something else. The move fell apart and Johnny got the blame.

Unsurprisingly, results weren't going too well. Racing struggled in Europe. They only won one game in their group. They weren't much better in the league, either. The rough and tumble of French rugby was beginning to bite. Johnny started to wonder if he had made a mistake.

Go, Johnny, Go!

On good days, if they won, he felt on top of the world. Everything was easy. He thought he could be in Paris for the rest of his life. But after a defeat, he just wanted to get out of there. Move back to Dublin and be with his family and friends again. And Racing were losing more often than they were winning.

One day, out of the blue, Johnny got a call from home. It was ROG. He had retired the year before after a glorious career. Despite their early differences, Johnny and ROG had become good friends. Their respect for each other had grown. It was easier to be friends when they weren't in competition for the Ireland number 10 jersey.

'It looks like I might be joining you in Paris. As a coach,' said ROG.

Johnny thought he was joking at first. But he was serious. ROG wanted to get into coaching. Racing had offered him a deal to join as skills coach. Johnny wondered if ROG was going to follow him around for the rest of his life!

France

Johnny was delighted when ROG came to France. It was nice to have a familiar face from home around. Johnny and Laura became close friends with ROG and his wife, Jess. Life in Paris became a little easier.

A few weeks later, Johnny got another surprise. Laura told him she was expecting a baby. Johnny was going to become a dad. He was so excited. A new life in Paris and now he was going to start a family of his own. With a spring in his step, it was time to take a break from France to head back to Ireland for the start of the Six Nations.

Chapter 18
Six Nations glory

Johnny was so excited to come home to Ireland and meet up with his old teammates again for the start of the Six Nations. There had been a change at the top once more. Declan Kidney had moved on after last year's awful results. He had been replaced by Joe Schmidt, Johnny's old coach at Leinster. Johnny was delighted. They were back together again. They hoped to repeat their Leinster success with the national team.

Ireland's opening match was at home to Scotland at the Aviva Stadium. It couldn't have gone better. Tries from Andrew Trimble, Jamie Heaslip and Rob Kearney did the damage.

Six Nations glory

Johnny piled on the misery with five kicks from six. He was back on home soil in Dublin and back on form.

Next up came Wales in round two. This was always a tricky test for Ireland. But not today. Schmidt had the team flying and they soon put the Welsh away. Johnny continued his fine kicking form with another five from six in a 26-3 win. Everyone was starting to get excited. Could they win the Triple Crown? The Six Nations? The Grand Slam? There was a long way to go yet.

A tricky trip to Twickenham to play England soon put an end to the hype. Ireland were choked by England's strong defence. Johnny did what he could to break them down. He tried all the tricks in his playbook. A try from Rob Kearney looked like it would decide the game. But England fought back. Johnny kicked another penalty, before England came again. A try from Danny Care gave England a 13-10 win. So much for the Grand Slam. Johnny was disappointed. Ireland were down but not out.

Go, Johnny, Go!

They still had two more games. They were still in the hunt for the Championship.

The next match against Italy was Drico's last game for Ireland at home. It was all anyone could talk before the game. They were selling 'BOD' scarves outside the stadium. Everyone wanted to wave goodbye to Ireland's greatest ever rugby player. There's no way Ireland were losing this one. Johnny made sure of that.

He took just seven minutes to set Ireland on their way. Ireland had all the ball and were building pressure. Drico picked up the ball and released Johnny with a typical piece of skill.

Try! Johnny Sexton!

His second came right on the hour mark. O'Driscoll was at the heart of it. The Kearney brothers got involved, too. Rob to Dave to Johnny.

Try! Sexton gets a second. Ireland are home and dry!

Ireland cut loose after that. They finished up with 46-7. Johnny had pitched in with 17

Six Nations glory

points himself. It was the perfect send-off for Drico. He deserved it.

They didn't celebrate yet. They still had work to do. Their final game was a trip to Paris to play France on St Patrick's weekend. Johnny was returning to his new home with the Six Nations title on the line. The French were sure to greet him with a special welcome.

Johnny was more hyped than usual in the run-up to this one. He really wanted to put on a show in front of the French fans. It was another emotional day in the Irish dressing room. It was Drico's last match. He gave an inspiring speech and sent the players onto the field with their hearts pumping.

France made the better start. Johnny's Racing Métro teammate Machenaud put them 6-0 up with two penalties. But Johnny dragged Ireland back into the match. After huge work from the forwards, Chris Henry popped up with the ball close to the line. He flipped a back-handed pass out to Johnny. Johnny dropped his shoulder and turned on the gas. He headed straight for the line.

Go, Johnny, Go!

Try for Ireland! Johnny Sexton!

Johnny threw the ball into the air in delight.

'Yes, Johnny! Come on!' shouted Drico.

They were back in the match.

Then they went in front.

This time, Murray found space through the middle. He popped the ball to Andrew Trimble. Trimble showed a quick pair of feet to finish.

Try! Trimble! Are Ireland on their way to the title?

Not if France could help it. The Blues got past Ireland's defence for another try. Ireland were behind again at half-time, 13-12. Johnny missed an easy kick in front of the posts. He was furious with himself. The crowd whistled and jeered.

As the French fans sang 'Allez les Bleus', Paul O'Connell laid down the law just before the start of the second half.

'We've come this close before. Don't let it slip today. Do it for Drico!' he said as he thumped his fist into his hand.

The pressure was on.

Six Nations glory

France were all over Ireland again. Squeezing them up front. Just when his teammates needed him most, Drico pulled another moment of magic out of the bag. He made a brilliant break upfield, but he was caught just short of the line. The ball popped back up to Johnny, just a few metres from the line. He made no mistake to touch down.

Johnny Sexton with his second try! Look how much it means to him!

Johnny added another penalty. Ireland were nine points ahead. A fairytale ending was in sight. But it's never that simple. France piled forward once more. They powered their way over for another try. It was 22-20 now. A gripping game. Nobody could take their eyes off it. Everyone back home in Ireland was glued to the television.

Johnny looked up at the scoreboard. There was still 20 minutes left. How would they hold on? France were smashing Ireland with wave after wave. The men in green were standing firm. It was epic. With seconds left

Go, Johnny, Go!

on the clock, Ireland finally cracked. They got caught too narrow and the flying French went wide. Damien Chouly touched down. Ireland thought they were done for. Their dreams were crushed. Johnny put his head in his hands.

But then came a lifeline. The referee checked the video replay. He had seen a forward pass. The try was disallowed.

Ireland defended like their lives depended on it. The clock ticked down. Every second felt longer and longer. Finally, the referee blew his whistle.

That's it! It's over! Ireland have hung on! Ireland are the Six Nations champions!

A glorious end to a glorious career for Brian O'Driscoll!

The stadium fell dark. Ireland walked up to collect the trophy. Paul O'Connell stood beaming from ear to ear. Drico was beside him. Two legends of Irish rugby. A huge blast of fireworks went off. The sky lit up. Johnny stared on in disbelief as the trophy went into

Six Nations glory

the air. Ireland had done it. Johnny had done it. He had finally achieved his dream with Ireland. They were finally the Six Nations champions.

Chapter 19
In the wars

By the next summer, Johnny was celebrating again. This time it had nothing to do with rugby. His first son, Luca, was born in June. It was the happiest day of his life. He was so excited to return to Paris to continue his adventure with his new family.

The good news just kept coming. Shortly afterwards, he found out he had been nominated for World Player of the Year. There were just five players on the list. The others were All Blacks Brodie Retallick and Julian Savea and Springboks Willie le Roux and Duane Vermeulen. Johnny always cared about winning matches and trophies with his team

In the wars

more than personal awards. But he had to admit, it was an amazing feeling to be seen as one of the best in the business.

There was no time for him to reflect on the glory, though. He was straight into the start of the new season for Racing Métro. He was at the heart of the action. They beat Montpellier but then lost to Bordeaux. He was getting plenty of attention now and was in the wars week after week. The opposition knew he was the danger man. They were targeting him with some big hits. The next match was a big win over Toulon at home. Johnny took another heavy blow from a late shoulder charge.

Owwwww!

A broken jaw. He could hardly eat for days with the pain. Even worse, he was out of action for six weeks.

But Johnny was soon back on his feet. Ireland's November internationals were about to start. He easily kept up his brilliant run of form. He was Man of the Match in a huge win over the Springboks. He had mixed his kicking

Go, Johnny, Go!

and running game to perfection in a 29-15 win for Ireland. But he suffered another big hit right at the end. He was starting to get used to this.

Johnny played another starring role a week later in a breathless game against Australia. The moment of the match came just 12 minutes in. Rory Best pulled off a huge turnover in midfield. Johnny had a look at the space and decided to launch one high into the corner.

What a kick! It's inch perfect from Sexton. Zebo is chasing it. Zebo is going to get there!

Try!

Ireland raced into a 17-0 lead. The Aussies fought back in a hugely physical match. Johnny defended like a lion. He put his body on the line time and again. Right at the end, Johnny smacked heads with his own teammate Rob Kearney.

Owwwww!

He was out of it. He had to come off. Thankfully, Ireland held on in the closing

In the wars

stages for a 26-23 win. But it was bad news for Johnny.

He suffered headaches and dizzy spells for weeks after the game. He wasn't feeling well at all. He went to see a specialist doctor in Paris.

'I'm OK most of the time. I can get through a couple of training sessions no bother,' Johnny told him. 'But sometimes I just feel dizzy and I have headaches.'

'Your body has been through a lot, Johnny,' the doctor told him. 'I think it's best if you take a rest. I don't think you should play any rugby for 12 weeks.'

'12 weeks?' Johnny replied with horror. 'But I'll miss the start of the Six Nations!'

'Your health is the most important thing, Johnny,' said the doctor.

Johnny knew he was right.

He missed the opening Six Nations win over Italy. But he was back, refreshed and ready to go, for Ireland's second game against France in Dublin on St Valentine's Day. It was like he was never away. He had a perfect game. He kicked

Go, Johnny, Go!

five from five as Ireland won 18-11. Their next match was against England at the Aviva Stadium. Johnny had another stormer in a 19-9 win. He kicked five from six, adding to Robbie Henshaw's try. Ireland had now won three in a row. Johnny was feeling great. He had no headaches or pain.

A tricky away trip to Wales came soon after. Ireland gave their all. Johnny kicked four from five once again. But they narrowly lost out 23-16. Their Grand Slam hopes were over. They still had a chance to win the Six Nations in their last game against Scotland. There was huge excitement in Edinburgh before the match. Thousands of fans had arrived hoping to witness history.

Paul O'Connell gave a speech in the dressing room.

'We're on the brink of history,' he told the players. 'We can win two Six Nations in a row. Not many players can say that. Let's go out and make sure of it. Give everything. Don't let it slip,' he roared.

In the wars

Johnny could feel the energy pumping through his veins. He just wanted to get on the pitch.

Ireland made a great start. Captain O'Connell led by example as he crossed the line after just four minutes.

Try!

'Yes, Paulie!' Johnny shouted, as he patted him on the head. 'That's the start we needed!'

Johnny was in the mood and there was no stopping Ireland. They scored three more tries and Johnny added 18 points with the boot in a thumping 40-10 win. But there were no celebrations on the pitch. Not yet.

Ireland still had to wait for results elsewhere on a day that became known as Super Saturday. The players watched the final England v France game on TV in the dressing room at the stadium. It was such a strange feeling. Johnny and his teammates were shouting and screaming at the TV as a thrilling game played out in Paris. Finally, the whistle blew and they could celebrate.

Go, Johnny, Go!

Ireland are Six Nations champions again! Two in a row!

The players went wild. They jumped up and down. Ireland had spent years wanting to win the Six Nations. Now two had come along in a row!

Amid the celebrations, Johnny started to think of home and how much it meant to him. He loved playing with his friends. He loved having his family close by. Now that he had a son, he thought of how he would like him to come along to the RDS and see him playing for Leinster every week. He decided it was time to leave France and come back home to Ireland.

A deal was done with Irish Rugby. There was no messing this time. Johnny was happy with his contract and wasted no time signing it. The best out-half in the world was on his way home to Ireland and his boyhood team, Leinster. He had loved his time in Paris. But home is always home. There's no place like it.

Chapter 20
England 2015

It was another busy summer for Johnny. As well as packing his bags and saying goodbye to his teammates in Paris, he began preparations for the 2015 World Cup in England. As two-time Six Nations champions, Ireland travelled to England as one of the favourites. For the first time in Irish rugby history, the players really felt they could win the World Cup. Johnny believed it more than most.

They had a perfect draw. They started with winnable games against Canada, Romania and Italy. If everything went to plan, it would all come down to the final group decider against France. Johnny was in good spirits before the

Go, Johnny, Go!

tournament. He had a feeling it was going to go well.

It was a beautiful day in Cardiff for their first game of the tournament. It was like the middle of summer. Thousands of Irish fans had painted the town green. It was like a home match for Ireland. On the way to the stadium Johnny could see all the fans gathering and having fun. He spotted one couple with Canadian flags painted on one cheek and Irish flags on the other. It was a carnival atmosphere.

As kick-off approached, Johnny said a few words in the dressing room.

'We set our standards today. We have to win and win well. This is just the start. We'll have bigger games ahead, but we play today just as we would play a final.' He clapped his hands in support. 'Come on!'

It took Ireland 13 minutes to get going but once they did, they were unstoppable. Johnny kicked a penalty and then the tries started to flow. Seán O'Brien, Iain Henderson and then,

England 2015

just before the half-hour, Johnny got in on the act. O'Brien burst through the middle and confused the Canadian defence with an inside pass. Johnny was free, but he had a long way to go to the try line.

Sexton! Breaking through the middle. He's in so much space. It's a race to the line now. Does he have the pace? Yes he does!

Try! Johnny Sexton!

They finished with seven tries, a final score of 50-7. Ireland were up and running.

The very next day, back home, the All-Ireland football final was taking place between Dublin and Kerry. Divided loyalties for Johnny. He watched the match from the comfort of his hotel room, recovering after a job well done. Dublin and Kerry were his two favourite teams. It was hard to pick when they played each other. He was happy enough when Dublin won out by 12 points to 9.

Johnny was rested for the next game against Romania at Wembley Stadium, the

Go, Johnny, Go!

home of English football. When he was a young boy, Johnny always dreamed of scoring the winning goal there for Manchester United in the FA Cup final. He was disappointed not to be getting a run there. But he knew Ireland had bigger matches coming up and he needed to be fresh.

Ireland were easy winners again, this time 44-10. They were on a roll. Johnny was back for the next match against Italy. This would be another step up.

Sure enough, it was a tight, tough encounter. Italy are always hard to beat, especially at a World Cup. The game was held in the Olympic Stadium in London. Johnny looked around in awe as they entered the pitch. It was a spectacular place. In just two weeks, Ireland had played in two of the best stadiums in the world.

Keith Earls settled Ireland's nerves with a fine try after 20 minutes. Johnny had a couple of wobbles with the boot but he kicked three penalties and a conversion. They won out 16-9.

England 2015

It wasn't pretty and they could certainly have played better. But a win is a win. They were three from three and the mighty France were all that stood between them and a quarter-final.

They were back to Cardiff for this one. But the atmosphere was different. This game was serious. Ireland had been looking forward to it for at least a year. It meant more to Johnny than anyone else. Now that he was leaving Paris, people in France were saying that Johnny hadn't given his best for Racing Métro. That he hadn't been fully committed. That stung Johnny. He always gave everything on the pitch, no matter who he played for. He wanted to show everyone in France what they were missing. It was personal.

The atmosphere during the anthems was like nothing Johnny had seen before. The stadium roof was closed, which made it even louder than usual. Johnny got a shiver down his spine. No matter how many times he played for Ireland, he always felt a surge of pride when the anthems played.

Go, Johnny, Go!

It was a hugely physical game, as expected. Rugby is always a tough game. But this was war. The French were not happy that Johnny had decided to move home to Ireland. They were out to get him. Defences were on top early on. Johnny was coming in for some rough treatment. He started well and was striking the ball sweetly. He got two kicks in the opening 20 minutes to edge Ireland ahead. Suddenly, out of nowhere, disaster struck.

Smash! A huge hit from Louis Picamoles!

Johnny was down. And out. He limped off the pitch in despair. He buried his face in his jersey. He couldn't believe it. His World Cup dream was over.

Ireland went on to win the match, but it came at a huge cost. Paul O'Connell suffered a terrible injury and came off at half-time. His hamstring muscle ripped completely off the bone. An injury that would end his career. It was the last time the legend would ever play for Ireland. Peter O'Mahony was gone, too.

England 2015

Without their star trio, Ireland struggled in the quarter-final against Argentina. It was a day to forget. Ireland were given the run-around. Argentina were the better side and won out by 43 points to 20. It was more World Cup woe for Ireland. Four more years of hurt. The only upside for Johnny was that he was on his way home to Dublin to start his second spell at Leinster.

Chapter 21

Return to Leinster

Johnny was given a hero's welcome on his return to Leinster. It felt good to be back. His family slotted straight into life in Dublin. They were all happy to be home. It was like he had never left.

But on the pitch, things were a little different. Leinster had a new coach, Leo Cullen. Some of his old teammates had moved on. There was a new crop of young stars coming through, too. Among them was Joey Carbery. Carbery was a promising out-half, snapping at Johnny's heels. He hoped to win a place on the team, just as Johnny had done with ROG all those years before.

Return to Leinster

Things were not quite coming together on the pitch. Johnny felt the old standards had slipped. They were knocked out of Europe in the pool stages and results in the league were mixed. After a big 30-6 loss to Ulster, Johnny had seen enough. He decided to lay down the law.

'It's a pathetic scoreline. It's just not good enough. We have to turn it around,' he told his teammates. 'We have to get back to the level we were at. We can get there but we're a long way off.'

They knew he was right.

It wasn't going to be fixed overnight, but Johnny was determined to get Leinster back to their rightful place. They picked up a little to make the league final against Connacht. The outcome was a huge upset. Connacht pulled off one of the biggest shocks in Irish rugby. It was one of the worst days of Johnny's career. He knew Leinster had a big mountain to climb to get back to the top.

Go, Johnny, Go!

It was a season to forget with Ireland, too, in that year's Six Nations. Johnny played all five matches, but they lost to England and France and drew with Wales. He wondered if he would ever see the glory days again.

He didn't feel down for long, though. The day after the Wales game, his second child was born. Laura gave birth to baby Amy. A beautiful little girl. Johnny was so happy.

After spending plenty of time with his family over the summer, Johnny was ready to go for the new season. Leinster were learning from the harsh lessons. Johnny could see the young players getting better under his influence. Their first big test was a clash against old rivals Munster at the Aviva Stadium. It was to become a special day for Johnny.

Two tries in the first half meant Leinster were well in control. Early in the second half, Johnny stood over a penalty that would make him Leinster's all-time leading points scorer. He went through his routine as normal. He started his run up. He stuck it straight between the posts.

Return to Leinster

There it is! That's 1,228 points in the blue of Leinster for the one and only Johnny Sexton!

Johnny had beaten Felipe Contepomi's record as Leinster's top points scorer. What a feeling! Johnny thought back to the early days, when he thought he would never get past Felipe into the Leinster team. He felt so proud.

Leinster won the game and Johnny was named Man of the Match. After the game, he met his dad and they shared a big hug.

'I'm so proud of you, son,' he said with a tear in his eye.

Johnny played some of the best rugby of his career that season. He was at the top of his game. Leinster were improving all the time, too. They topped their pool in Europe and then thumped Wasps in the quarter-final, before narrowly losing the semi-final to French giants Clermont. They suffered a similar outcome in the league, too. They lost to Scarlets at home in the semi-final. It was awful to lose two semi-finals in one season. At least Johnny knew that

Go, Johnny, Go!

Leinster were back on track. He was getting older now. But he still felt the best was yet to come.

Chapter 22
Grand Slam glory

Johnny was about to play the season of his life. Ireland were one of the best teams in the world now. They feared nobody going into the Six Nations. They had set their sights on winning the Grand Slam. The almost impossible task of beating England, Wales, Scotland and France in one season. In more than 100 years they had only ever done it twice.

First up was the famous night in Paris when Johnny scored 'le drop goal'.

Sexton shows his guts and goes for glory!

Johnny stretched out his arms wide. He pumped his fists in the air. He couldn't believe

Go, Johnny, Go!

it. He'd done it. One of the greatest kicks of all time. It was his greatest moment on a rugby field.

The Ireland players celebrated long into the night in Paris. They were only getting started. Next up, they smashed Italy. Johnny kicked five from five.

Sexton on song!

Then came a bonus-point win over Wales at the Aviva. The final score was 37-27.

Sexton! Fizzing a skip pass out to Stockdale! Try!

Johnny then kicked four from four against Scotland.

Jacob Stockdale with two terrific tries!

It all came down to a Grand Slam decider against England. At Twickenham. On St Patrick's Day.

England had won 14 matches in a row at home. This was going to be tough. Johnny was nervous all week. He wasn't enjoying the build-up. This was one of the biggest matches of his life.

Grand Slam glory

It was freezing in London on the day of the match.

'It's so cold, even the polar bears are wearing a second pair of socks,' laughed Johnny's uncle Billy, as he made his way to the ground with Johnny's dad. Back home in Dublin, his mam left her hair salon in Rathgar to be home just in time for the start of the match. In Listowel, his nana Brenda was glued to the TV. They were all nervous.

With minutes to go to kick-off, Johnny spoke in the dressing room.

'It's all going to come down to today. This is our biggest challenge by far. We have a chance to make history!'

Even during the warm-up, steam was rising from the players because of the cold. But by kick-off, Johnny didn't feel it anymore. He was only focused on the game.

'Let's go, boys!' he roared, clapping his hands just before kick-off.

He was right into the action after just six minutes, starting a move that led to a try.

Go, Johnny, Go!

Sexton with a huge kick high into the snowy sky. Ringrose touches down as the ball bobs over the line.

Try!

Ireland were in front, thanks to Johnny again. Soon it was 14-0. A sweet pass from Tadhg Furlong set up CJ Stander.

Try!

Johnny pointed to the post. He raised both arms in the air. Ireland were on their way to a grand slam. But England weren't giving up. Johnny was right in the firing line.

Smash!

Johnny got a bang to the head. It didn't look good.

'I don't need to come off,' he roared at the referee. But he had no choice. The medics had to drag him off.

After a quick check he was soon back on. Johnny wasn't giving up that easily. Ireland had one hand on history now. They defended like their lives depended on it. England threw everything at them. But Ireland held strong to

Grand Slam glory

win 24-15. The final whistle was sweet music to Johnny's ears.

They've done it! Ireland are Grand Slam champions for just the third time in more than 100 years!

The celebrations were wild. Fireworks crackled and streamers fell to the ground. Captain Rory Best lifted the cup high into the cold night sky. Johnny smiled from ear to ear. He and Peter O'Mahony raised the Triple Crown shield. They huddled together on the pitch.

'That was pure courage, boys!' Joe Schmidt told the players, as he congratulated them on their achievement. 'I'm massively proud of every one of you.'

He saved his biggest hug for Johnny. His leader on the field. His general.

The party continued in the dressing room. Bundee Aki made a bodhrán out of a tray as they sang and danced. Johnny celebrated so much he lost his medal. He didn't care. They had given it everything. It was all worth it for this magic moment.

Go, Johnny, Go!

Johnny and his teammates were buzzing when they got back to Leinster. They wanted to finish out the season in style. Somehow, he found the energy to lead Leinster to yet another European Crown in Bilbao, Spain, in May. Leinster beat Scarlets too and collected the league title at home in the RDS. A double. The perfect season.

It gave Johnny great satisfaction. Ireland had won the Grand Slam. His boyhood club Leinster were back where they belonged as kings of Europe. Later that summer, his third child was born. Another beautiful baby girl. They named her Sophie. It was an amazing year. He thought things couldn't get much better. But he was wrong. There was one more night of glory to come.

***

Dublin was crackling with excitement all week. It was always special when the All Blacks came to town. Ireland had beaten New Zealand for the first time ever in Chicago in 2016. They

Grand Slam glory

had been playing them since 1905! Now, they wanted to beat them on home soil. They felt they had a chance.

It was a frosty November night. The fans were fizzing as the All Blacks entered the Aviva Stadium. They knew Ireland were up for this. Everyone could feel it in the air.

The All Blacks performed the famous Haka to startling silence inside the stadium. Then came the roar. It sent a shiver down Johnny's spine. The Irish fans broke out in a rousing rendition of 'The Fields of Athenry'. This was going to be a night to remember. Johnny could sense it.

He gave a last-minute talk to the team on the pitch.

'They're nothing special. We saw that with the Lions last summer. If we go after them, we can beat them. Come on!'

The whistle blew and the game was on.

Johnny struck an early penalty right in front of the posts. It was an easy settler. There wasn't much between them. Ireland were looking comfortable, but couldn't find

Go, Johnny, Go!

a way through. The All Blacks were always dangerous.

Ireland were just three points ahead early in the second half when Johnny spotted an opportunity. What followed was one of the greatest moments in Irish rugby history.

All week they had practised the move. Coach Joe Schmidt had noticed a weakness in the All Black defence. Johnny decided now was the time to make the most of it. Off the top of a line-out, the ball spun out to Johnny. He pulled the trigger. He pretended to go right but he cleverly moved the ball left.

Sexton switches back inside to Aki. Now the race is on. Stockdale!

Try!

'Yes!' Johnny roared, as the try-scoring machine Jacob Stockdale touched down the ball. He knew they wouldn't slip up now. They were about to make history once again. They just had to hold on with dogged defending. Finally, the relief of the referee's whistle could be heard. The crowd erupted.

Grand Slam glory

Ireland's dream comes true! They've beaten the All Blacks on home soil for the first time ever!

It was an amazing night. They were now ranked as the number one team in the world.

To top it all off, Johnny was nominated for World Player of the Year once more. A few weeks later, he travelled to a special ceremony in Monte Carlo with Laura. They got all dressed up for the glitzy night. All the best players in the world were there. Ireland were named Team of the Year. Joe Schmidt won the Coach of the Year Award. Then it came to the big moment. World Player of the Year. Johnny was nervous as the presenter on stage opened the envelope.

And the World Player of the Year for 2018 is Jonathan Sexton!

Johnny couldn't believe it. He was finally seen as the best in the world.

He had to pinch himself as he walked to the stage. After all the ups and downs, the self-doubt and the giving out. After the flawless

Go, Johnny, Go!

kicks and the bruising bumps. Johnny had risen above even his own wildest dreams. He thought back to his younger days, when he watched his dad playing for Bective and had scraps with his brothers on the green. And the days he dreamed of becoming Roy Keane, playing for Manchester United. He remembered his first steps on the rugby pitch. The time he smashed the lights in the ballroom at Bective Rugby Club. He thought of the days in Listowel, banging his ball against the wall. His schooldays at St Mary's, where he learned his trade and won the Senior Cup with a drop goal. He remembered when he thought he would never make it at Leinster. His battles with ROG to make Ireland's number 10 shirt his own. He thought of all the hard days, the injuries, the defeats and setbacks. Everything that had made him the player he had become. The Six Nations wins. The World Cup disappointments. The Grand Slam. The first ever win over the All Blacks. He had married Laura, the girl he loved when he was a boy. Now they had three

Grand Slam glory

beautiful children. Luca, Amy and Sophie. All his dreams had come true.

The little boy from Rathgar, whose jersey once hung over his knees, was now known all over the world as the greatest player in the game.